THE
NAKED SALON

An essential guide to time, team and money for salon owners

LISA CONWAY

Published by Zing Office in 2018.
Second Edition published 2016.
First Published 2014.

© Lisa Conway 2018

All rights reserved. The moral right of the author has been asserted. No part of this book may be reproduced by any person or entity, including internet search engines or retailers, in any form or by any means, electronic or mechanical, including photocopying (except under the statutory exceptions provisions of the Australian Copyright Act 1968), recording, scanning or by any information storage retrieval system without the prior written permission of the publisher.

National Library of Australia Cataloguing-in-Publication entry
Creator: Conway, Lisa, author.

Title: The naked salon: an essential guide to time, team and money for salon owners / Lisa Conway.

ISBN: 978-0-6480162-2-9 (pbk.)

Subjects: Beauty shops--Australia--Management.
Hairdressing--Australia--Management
Success in business--Australia.

Dewey Number: 646.72420681

Disclaimer
The material in this publication is of the nature of general comment only, and does not represent professional advice. It is not intended to provide specific guidance for particular circumstances and it should not be relied on as the basis for any decision to take action or not take action on any matter which it covers. Readers should obtain professional advice where appropriate, before making any such decision. The author and publisher disclaim all responsibility and liability to any person, arising directly or indirectly from any person taking or not taking action based on the informaton in this publication.

Front Cover photography: Jason Malouin www.portraitstore.com.au
Back Cover photography: www.unboundphotography.com.au
Editing: www.hiltoncopy.com
Front Cover design: www.thesqueezebox.com.au
Internal page layout: www.thesqueezebox.com.au
Last page design: Sarah Garner www.dmoguru.net
Illustrations: www.holopress.net
Printing: ExcitePrint www.exciteprint.com.au

To Simon,
Not only do you let me be myself
– you encourage it!

CONTENTS

Foreword		9
Preface		11
1	Why on Earth should you listen to my advice?	17
2	Business basics: a quick overview	27
3	Simple systems that make your life easy and deliver consistent results	35
4	Setting goals that lead to satisfaction	53
5	Leading your team to success	65
6	Building, nurturing and motivating your team	83
7	Mystery shoppers, quality control and confidence	103
8	Setting expectations and training your team	115
9	Knowing and growing your average dollar sale	125
10	Knowing exactly how much money you need to break even	139
11	How much are your discounts really costing you?	151
12	You wouldn't just 'guess' your colour proportions, would you?	
13	The 3 'R's: Rebooking, Recommending and Retail	179

CONTENTS

14	Simple marketing that works for you	191
15	How to 'Wow' your clients all the way to the till!	201
16	Unhappy clients, bad clients and common mistakes	217
17	Creative solutions that make your clients spend more with a smile	233
18	Clients belong to the salon, not the staff	245
19	A-grade clients make your life a joy – but you may not recognise them at first glance	255
20	Why did you buy a salon in the first place?	265

> *"The best time to plant a tree is twenty years ago.
> The second best time is now."*
>
> Unknown

FOREWORD

If you're reading this book, you should be thrilled for what's about to happen. Everything is about to change. You'll never think about your business in the same way again. This is our story …

When we first met Lisa a couple of years ago, we wondered what she could offer us. Little did we know the amazing journey she was about to take us on.

With 29 salons and a 120-strong team, we had a good business and a great team. Or so we thought. You don't know what you don't know. We were too close to our problems to even get that we had problems.

Lisa changed all that. She listened patiently and challenged our thinking. She helped us identify and work on our strengths and weaknesses. Together, we learnt not to settle for mediocrity but aspire to excellence.

Lisa's layers of learnings are incredible. It's like a multi-tiered rainbow cake. How she knows when to release the next layer is a mystery. It's as though she reads your mind and knows what you're ready for next.

At times, Lisa was brutally honest. She'd walked in our shoes and totally understood our struggles. Her years of industry knowledge and personal experience on the ground means she can tell it how it is and back it with facts – all without the fluff or BS. It's exactly what we needed to gain clarity and become confident leaders.

Consistency across our multiple locations and sizable team was our biggest challenge. Lisa taught us how to put robust systems in place. Now, whether we have 2, 20 or 200 salons, we're all working in sync. It's given us the solid foundation we needed to expand our brand nationally.

Lisa has a unique way of bringing out your best. She's helped us grow professionally and personally. We have evolved into better versions of ourselves.

There's so much to love about Lisa – her kind-heartedness, humour, authenticity and honesty are the icing on the cake. Her desire to help others is genuine and she continues to inspire us every day.

It's not until you look back at how far you've come that you really appreciate the scale of the business mountain you've climbed. There's no way we'd be reaching these heights without Lisa's incredible insights.

Sandrine Leven and Rizwan Syed
Founders – Zubias Threading
www.zubiasthreading.com.au

PREFACE

It's a beautiful morning and a public holiday here in Melbourne, just perfect for an early morning walk in the local park with my four legged darling, Muriel. She's a 'Schnoodle' (Poodle-Schnauzer cross), and one of the things she and I have in common is awesome curls.

Since I'm a hairdresser at the very core of my being, Muriel has an unusual hair-cut that makes her stand out. I use scissors to cut her hair, and all the same techniques we use to get very small children to behave during their haircuts. Anyway, most of the regular park visitors know Muriel by sight, and she gets a lot of admiring comments.

Muriel loves to go 'off-lead' and find her own playmates. Fellow 'poodle crosses' are usually her first choice; working dogs, like Kelpies, are not on her list (maybe they think she looks too much like a sheep, and try to herd her!).

Today Gypsy, a Guide Dog I often see, was off-lead and off-duty. Muriel started playing with him, so I took the opportunity to introduce myself to Gypsy's owner, whom I often see, but have never chatted to (since Gypsy is usually working and I don't want to distract him). I explained that I had seen the pair of them here before, but respected that her dog was working and I didn't want to interrupt. She thanked me for understanding that rule, and invited me to pat Gypsy, since he was off-duty.

I mentioned to the lady that over the years I have met some

fabulous working Labradors as Guide Dogs in my salons, and was in awe of the service they deliver every day. Then the conversation turned to 'my salon'. This lady had been looking for a great colourist for some time, as she wasn't happy with her hair. It was interesting that, even though she couldn't see it for herself, she wasn't happy with her hair colour. I explained that my career had taken me to another place, and that I was now coaching salon owners: teaching them how to do what they love and make it profitable (there being not much point having a beautiful salon and an ugly bank account!)

I offered to refer her to a salon that I thought would suit her, if she'd first answer a few questions. She agreed, and after a few minutes I was able to recommend a salon where I knew she would get what she needed. I started to explain why I thought this particular salon would be a good fit for her, and told her about the owner – a delightful man with a small family who has a passion for the Arts and is also an opera singer.

She smiled and said "Wow, so am I!"

The lady then asked me if I could put the salon's details into her phone so she could call them in the morning to make an appointment.

When I turned to check on the dogs, they were both sitting in the shade crunching on sticks, something Gypsy is not allowed to do, and Muriel never does. Just like children, they took the opportunity to do something forbidden, simply because we weren't watching! I am certain that Muriel (who can be terrible) had something to do with the idea.

I think that connecting with people and building relationships is the thing I love most about my career – it's certainly something I've always been good at. I sometimes think the hair and beauty industry chose me, rather than the other way around.

When I still worked on the floor, I would have given that lady my salon's name and looked after her hair personally. When I owned a salon, someone on my team would have taken care of her. Now that I'm a coach, I'm still finding the right connections and relationships for people. Now it's the salon that I mentor, rather than the staff.

After thirty years in the hair and beauty industry, not much has changed. I'm still listening to people so that I can deliver whatever is needed to make their salon experience awesome.

Which only goes to show… Once a hairdresser, always a hairdresser!

one

Why on Earth should you listen to my advice?

As you may have gathered from my Foreword, I'm a hairdresser to the very core of my being. I even take care of my dog's hair, and I help random people I meet in the park find the right person to help them take care of their hair.

In a minute I'll tell you a bit about myself and my love affair with the hair and beauty industry, so you can understand where I'm coming from and why I genuinely care about you and making your salon successful. But first I'd like to ask you a few questions, 'one salon owner to another':

Are you getting everything you want or expect from your salon? Does it give you time for the other things you want in your life?

Does it give you a fair return on the time, effort and money you invest in it?

Do you love it like you used to?

If the answer to all 4 of these questions is "Yes", then you might get a few ideas out of this book – and you'll probably find yourself nodding in agreement as you read. But if you answered "No" to even one of them, then I hope in this book you'll find the clues you need to create the life you need, with more time to yourself and the money to enjoy it.

So now let me tell you my story

I grew up on a farm in the Mallee as one of nine children. I never dreamed of being a hairdresser. In our small town there was a barber with a wooden leg, and one hairdresser – a bubbly, buxom blonde who I'll call Sandy – who had no time for my 'difficult' head of hair, but lots of time to talk about the locals or chat with my brother. Whenever I showed her styles in hair magazines, I was told "But you don't have the right hair for that". I was absolutely convinced that I had been dealt a bad head of hair and the best thing I could do was to cover it with a great hat!

In 1983 at the mature age of 18, I walked into a large salon in Elizabeth Street in Melbourne's CBD because I needed a haircut. I didn't know it at the time, but that simple decision would change my life forever.

The girl at the desk was so welcoming and genuinely interested in me and my hair. She asked me questions about it, such as "How often do you shampoo your hair?", "What do you want from your hair?", "How much time are you prepared to put in to achieve your look?" She took both me and my hair seriously.

1

She cut my hair into the style we had discussed, she spoke about colouring my hair in the future and went on to give me the best blow wave I had ever had, all the time explaining how I would be able to take better care of it with the knowledge she shared with me, such as: how to stretch the root area first; how to take most of the moisture out before I began; how to use clips to isolate the section I was working on; and how I would be able to complete my whole head in about 20 minutes if I just used these simple tips. I learned that I had a fabulous head of hair – I just didn't know how to care for it. The whole experience completely blew me away!

I walked out of the salon feeling a foot taller, and absolutely gorgeous from the inside out. I had experienced a hairdresser with passion!

Right there and then, I decided what I wanted to do with my life. I wanted to be like her. I wanted to make people feel beautiful, improve their day, solve their hair problems and create such an awesome atmosphere that people would queue for it.

So I enrolled in a one year course, passed at the top of my class and began my first job, where I worked as part of a big team in a busy shopping centre for the next sixteen years. I became the manager, and of course the boss's favourite because I never took a sick day and was always booked up. I met my targets and loved sharing my knowledge, just like the girl in Elizabeth Street.

1

Do you remember what motivated you to become a hairdresser? Do you recall that feeling of loving what you were doing?

I remember it like it was yesterday, but it hasn't always been easy to hang on to. Somewhere in along the way, what seemed to be a 'happily ever after' ending gradually changed. Over the years, it became 'bums in seats', and customer care ran second to speed. I was well paid, but my job satisfaction had slipped so I decided it was time to move on.

In a brave moment in 2001, I opened my first salon. I didn't have a single client, but I knew I could build up a clientele quickly. It was so exciting, fitting out the salon and choosing the paint. I was in heaven! My energy was infectious and my staff of one quickly grew to five. I was making all the decisions and I loved it.

But, you know, it wasn't easy keeping all the balls in the air while juggling three kids and a husband. I was so tired and I hadn't had a real break in years. I'd manage a week off here and there, but I'd have to do a truck load of work before I could get away, and when I returned it was all piled up again. If I wasn't there, the takings dropped, and I was sick of training new staff and then having them leave just when they were filling the appointment book.

My attitude was starting to show in my work. 'Near enough' was creeping in, and I was slipping into a 'Sandy': just getting through my work and chatting about the latest movies and events rather than taking my clients seriously.

Is this where you are now? Struggling, looking after everyone else (both staff and clients), putting yourself last... and thinking "Who signed me up for this?"

Let me tell you how I learned to love my career again

Two things happened: I met and worked with a Business Coach named Bruce; and I learnt the value of marketing – I realised you can't just do a great job and hope clients will mention to friends how great you are. These two things opened up a world of possibilities for me, and a new chapter in my career began to unfold.

> *I want to help you recover the passion and creativity you once had.*

For the first time in years I had someone to turn to: someone who was objective, concerned about my outcomes, and tough enough to hold me accountable. I didn't have to worry all weekend over a 'what if?' situation; nor did I have to solve all my problems alone. I had someone to talk things through with, and someone to challenge my thoughts.

Bruce asked me tough questions like "Why do you charge this for this service, but not that service?", "Why do you let that staff member come in at that time?" and "Why do you give that task to that team member?"

1

I learnt to question everything I did, and everything I thought I knew about running a salon. I learnt that in order to be a great leader I had to work harder on myself than on anyone else. I learnt about psychometric testing and the importance of knowing my own behavioural style as well as my team's. I learnt how to create an environment where the team works whether I'm there or not. How to assemble and develop a team of stylists and receptionists where everyone has clear roles and everyone is happy to be there. It was a steep learning curve!

However, I doubled my sales in twelve months and found that I no longer needed to be in the salon all the time. In fact, I no longer had to cut hair at all – our loyal clients could be wonderfully cared for by my enthusiastic and productive team. Then I received an offer for the salon too good to refuse. Since my needs had changed, I sold it and moved on, then went on to do the same thing again… and again. I realised I could apply these same principles to salons anywhere.

I had my life back. I had learned to love the beauty business again! And you know what happened next? Other salon owners started talking to me about their problems and asking me for help. I loved mentoring them. At first I was doing it informally, but then, as my first clients achieved success and recommended me to others, it turned into a full-time career. I love sharing my tools and knowledge with salon owners so that they can achieve the same kind of success that I, and my other clients, have had.

1

You know what? I know what it's like to struggle to pay the bills and still have something left over. I know what it's like when your staff are driving you crazy and you can't leave your salon for any length of time without something going wrong. I know what it's like to settle for a 'production line' – just getting those clients in and out again; losing that sense of achievement when they look at themselves and say "Wow!"

That isn't what you wanted when you went into the hair and beauty industry, is it? So I want to help you recover all the passion and creativity you once had – and that's what this book is about. It's not about being an award-winning salon, it's about creating the lifestyle you want, the money you want, and a team that makes every day a joyful new opportunity!

For more information and resources head to salonsmarts.work

two

2

Business basics: a quick overview

Imagine I'm your salon's Business Coach and we're sitting down together. Now the first thing that needs to happen is for me to learn a bit about you: where you are today, and where you'd like to be. Because, if I'm going to help you get your life back – just like I've got mine back – I need to know some things about you.

So, can I ask "How are you?" No really, how **ARE** you?
Does your salon drain the life out of you?
Are you being paid what you're worth?
When did you last have a real break, leaving the salon with someone you trust?
How are your rebooking rates?
How are your retail sales?
Do you plan to sell one day?
Do you know what your salon is worth?
Are you making the best use of your floor space?
Does everyone in your team love what they're doing?
Do you really love what you're doing?
If not, I can help you learn to love it again.

2

Unlike other Business Coaches, I am one of you - an experienced salon owner. I've had a wonderful career and it's time to share what I've learned. I'm still in the industry and I still have the same struggles as you – I've just learned the strategies to turn those challenges (big and small) into successes.

I can show you how you can move to a better place financially; how you can afford to get your life back while still having a successful business that you can be proud of. Of course, it will take effort on your part. But if you're prepared to make changes… then I can help you do it faster, better and more smoothly.

My business philosophy is to work *smarter*, not harder!

You'll get all the details in chapters dedicated to each essential element of running a successful hair or beauty salon as a business, but getting your life back boils down to dealing with three key aspects:

Your **Time:** Setting goals, establishing priorities, creating a lifestyle business

Your **Team:** Choosing them, leading them, training them, motivating them

Your **Money:** Paying your bills, reducing waste, increasing your profits

You might wonder why 'Your Clients' aren't mentioned. Well, they're a core part of the business and you'll hear plenty about them, too.

Are you making any of these 7 mistakes?

Week after week I talk to salon owners who are making them, so if your answer is "Yes", you're not alone!

Time

1. Are you too 'busy being busy' to work on your business?
2. Do you have systems in place so that things get done the way you like it, whether you are there or not?

Team

3. Do you have regular one-on-one meetings and team meetings to build your team's morale?
4. Are you leading your team, and training them to be better than you are in certain areas?

Money

5. Do you understand your break even numbers, and measure team performance?
6. Are you controlling your stock budget and waste?
7. Are you effectively and efficiently marketing your business?

This is just a snippet of the knowledge I have to share with you. I haven't even started on how to attract, retain and motivate fabulous staff. They're out there, believe me! You probably have some excellent people on your team right now. I can show you how to unearth their potential, how to develop the team you deserve, and how to protect yourself from the loss when they move on.

Then there's goal setting, strategic marketing and creating promotions that work. We have a lot to work on!

It's taken me a full career to accumulate what I know about operating successful salons, and I haven't finished learning yet. I'm continually researching and analysing; visiting salons and seeing what they're doing right, what they're doing wrong, what's working and what's not.

I've given myself the time to really think about and develop strategies and techniques that make a genuine difference in salon environments, and I'm sharing a lot of what I know here. If you read this book carefully you'll learn the essential business skills every salon owner needs, but none of us were taught.

For more information and resources head to salonsmarts.work

> *"If you read this book carefully you'll learn the essential business skills every salon owner needs, but none of us were taught."*

three

3

Simple systems that make your life easy and deliver consistent results

3

The hair and beauty industry struggles with a lot of problems as a direct result of a lack of systems and clear guidelines. Because there is little clarity on what's expected, we just repeat the same instructions over and over, but it really doesn't have to be that way. We need to create clear systems for everything from how we expect our staff to appear and behave, to how our treatments are carried out; from what happens when a person walks into the salon, right through every kind of treatment, until the time when they pay and leave the salon.

If we set out clear instructions for our team right from the moment they start working with us – and display our points of culture in the lunch room – then everyone knows what to expect, and we don't need to keep going over the same ground.

In the corporate world, or in institutions like schools, they have paperwork for the paperwork. This ensures that everyone knows what is expected of them. I certainly don't expect you to do that in our industry. However, I do suggest you do a little more than you are doing right now – you can use my 'Fix it Once' method and move on to the next thing on your list. Your paperwork shows what you have decided about certain points of your salon culture. If you do your paperwork now, you won't waste energy repeating yourself, and you'll have more energy for the things that matter.

There are two main areas of these standards, **Team Culture** and **Servicing Clients**, and we'll look at some ways of clarifying both. I want to stress that I firmly believe that **posters** are much more effective than a Salon Manual (most of these are so long-winded, I fall asleep around page 4). The funniest rule I found in a Salon Manual was "No drinking while working in the salon." I highlighted it and showed it to the owner (who is one of my favourite clients) because I know she likes to have a drink after 5pm. Her reply was priceless: "Well, they drive me to drink, and I only do it on late nights when I've earned it. Anyway, it's meant for the team, not for me and I put it in a coffee mug so nobody knows I'm drinking."

It didn't matter, because nobody read the manual, so nobody knew that's what it said – but that's the point. There's no point making rules if no-one knows about them. If you really want a rule about drinking in the salon, make it plain and public: "I can drink in the salon, you can't." That way it's perfectly clear to everyone.

'Fix it Once'!

To 'Fix it Once' takes a little more effort at the start; however it will pay off over and over again. It doesn't just work for you, but for the team as well. They start to think about how to fix something the first time, so they don't have to ask over and over again.

It makes your life so much easier, because staff stop coming to you to ask about things like days off. For example, if someone asks "Can I have next Wednesday off?" your answer should be "What is the salon policy?" If the salon policy says they must give three weeks notice, or they can't have a single day so must take the week as annual leave – then there is the answer. Better yet, the policy will say that they need to have completed an application form from the second drawer of the filing cabinet. Now you could include a clause that says "In exceptional circumstances, please make your request in writing", and even outline what an exceptional circumstance might look like, so everyone is clear. There is always an exception to all the guidelines in the world, and I call it the 'fire and blood' rule: if there is a fire or blood, then it's an exception.

It beats the game of 'trying to get you on a good day'. When my daughter was three years old, my sister asked her "Who is the toughest, Mummy or Daddy?" and she looked my sister straight in the eye and said "When Mummy says 'no' it's 'no', but when Daddy says 'no' there's still a chance." She was just three at the time! It certainly bit her father more than once when he had a whining child following him around the supermarket saying "Go on Dad, why can't we? Please, please." And more often than not he said "Yes", just to keep them quiet. That's what she meant by "there's still a chance".

3

Once, when my three kids were in primary school, they were chatting over dinner and the twins said their teacher had threatened to keep them in at lunch time for something they did (probably talking). They were rapt that he didn't follow through, and my daughter piped up and said "Nah. Don't worry. He always says stuff he doesn't follow through with."

It was this teacher's second year teaching. He had my daughter the first year and then my twin sons the second. The poor chap hadn't counted on me ticking him off for not keeping kids in! I made a time to see him after I dropped the kids off, and I told him about the conversation at our dinner table. He apologised profusely, and I said "Don't apologise, just keep them in today. And my tip is: If you say it, then mean it!" My kids were terribly disappointed when two days later he remembered and actually kept them in (they never knew I'd tipped him off). I hear that he is still teaching, so I can't have scared him off too badly. My intention was to save him a lot of time, and it's the same in the salon.

Say what you mean, mean what you say – and never be mean when you say it. If you go with the 'Fix it Once' thinking, you will move on to the next issue and stop chasing your tail.

I had a rule about phone interruptions while I was working on the salon floor. I loved my time with the scissors and already got interrupted enough by the team, so I certainly didn't want to be interrupted any more than necessary. My kids would call the shop and convince the person who answered the phone to "get Mum, please". I would shout out "Is there a fire?" And my son would then say "It's OK, I guess it can wait until later."

This firm policy made it easy for me when friends or family of my team just 'popped in' to the salon. Our policy was to stop what you were doing, greet them at the front door and say "It's lovely to see you, but I can't talk right now, I'm with a client." (In their own time they could explain that the salon's policy is not to interrupt). If everyone knows the rules, everyone – including the owner – can follow them and there's nothing more to say.

> *Say what you mean, mean what you say – and never be mean when you say it*

If you follow through with this 'Fix it Once' thinking, it's amazing how much time you can free up, and you will stop feeling like a scratched record.

It's interesting that a lot of the time I'd find myself being the umpire between the staff and the owner. Your staff member doesn't lie in bed at night thinking "How can I annoy my boss?

I know – I'll just leave the lid off the peroxide tomorrow!" It's just not that important to them. So you need to make it important to them – and whining under your breath while putting the lid back on yourself fixes nothing! Work out the 'who', and ask them to come back to the bottle and pop the lid on... "please". The extra effort it takes makes it sink in, and it won't happen again.

Let me explain how I worked this one out. One day when I arrived to pick up the twins from kinder, Aaron ran across the room very excited to see his Mummy (like he was surprised I returned!) The kindergarten teacher quietly said "Aaron, we don't run at kinder do we? So please, go back to the other side of the room and walk over like we agreed."

His little face was the colour of a baboon's backside, but he did what he was told, and he never ran across the room again.

I learnt something very valuable that day.

If you take the time to explain things and get the person to correct their error, it will set in their mind like Ready Cement. I use that approach all the time.

Every client, every time!

One thing I must make absolutely clear is that you must service your clients the same every single time. It seems to be a big challenge for most salons, and since I know about the realities of salon life, I get why this happens. But I still say to my coaching clients: "Every client deserves the same consistent service, and they deserve it every time they come into your salon".

The only way to deliver this is to create a system for every process in your salon, and train every staff member to do each thing the same way. That way, whether your clients get Jenny or Jamie for their scalp treatment, they get the same experience. The reason for this is simple: your clients deserve the best treatment, and they need to have confidence they'll receive it whether you're having a busy day or a quiet one; whether Jenny's on holidays or not.

> *Every client deserves the same consistent service and they deserve it every time they come into your salon*

Let me tell you what often happens when I ask a salon owner "How long does a massage treatment at the basin take?"

I'll hear answers like "Anything from 1 minute to 5 minutes" or "It depends on who's doing it." Or even "It depends on how busy we are."

And my next questions will always be "Why isn't it clear? Why isn't there a set time and process?"

Of course, I know why. It's because sometimes you need to start a client right away, so you give the international signal for "Hurry the hell up!" At other times you are way behind, so you signal for "Take your time because I'm 'up shit creek in a barbed wire canoe', and if you stall for me I will love you forever." It doesn't matter where I am delivering this message, everyone laughs because we have all been guilty of this.

So, if you are short of time, do you leave the back of the head and only colour the front? Do you wax the front of the legs and leave the back? If you have loads of time, do you add unnecessary foils so it takes longer? Of course not! So why do you do this with your basin treatment? It's a service that deserves the same respect as all your other services, and if you and your team don't demonstrate that, your clients won't value them either.

> *"Systems are the answer to your problem"*

In beauty services, the weak point is those fabulous neck and shoulder massages which happen while a mask is doing its magic on your skin. Some therapists stay with you the whole time, while others disappear to find other tasks to do. It's your job as the salon owner to set out exactly what is expected for each service you offer. Your clients deserve consistent service, and if they don't get it, they get confused.

Let's say that Susan has come in and she's having her first deep conditioning hair and scalp treatment, which comes with a 3 minute scalp massage. This day the stylist has extra time, so she gives Susan a 6 minute massage instead. Susan is like soft butter after her beautiful massage and hair treatment, and all is wonderful in her world. So she rebooks and is looking forward to the same experience. But the next time she comes in, the salon has been having one of those crazy days, and the 3 minute massage lasts only 2 minutes. For Susan, it's gone from the 6 minute massage which she loved, to a 2 minute massage. Guess what? Susan feels cheated! It's really important to tell your clients if you are doing something extra for them.

So how do you give the same experience to every client, every time?

Systems are the answer to your problem. Now you may think that you're in the hair and beauty industry and systems don't apply, but the truth is we all can follow a system and you are already following quite a few. For example:

- Do you ever cut hair without covering the client with a wrap?
- Do you ever shampoo without using shampoo and conditioner?
- Do you ever do a facial without first removing your client's makeup?
- Do you ever answer the salon phone with "Yep, what's up bro?"

These are all systems, even if they are not written down anywhere.

Make a list of the things you won't compromise on in your salon.

- I always expected every member of my team to look up and smile when the door opened and a client walked in. "Hi" was a bonus, but everyone must look up and smile.
- Calling the client by their first name was another. Never "Come with me!" It had to be "Susan, would you like to come with me?"
- They had to clip the front of a towel with a butterfly clip every time they put one on. I didn't want towels falling on the floor half-way through the service!
- They had to ask every single client how they managed their hair in the morning and give at least one styling tip.

Not only did I have a system for each of these items, I also checked if that system was being carried out.

Most salons struggle to treat every client the same every time, and that's the biggest reason they fail to provide exceptional service and keep clients until they die or move away. Get this right, and you can't help being awesome (and profitable)!

Look, you either make excuses for inconsistent service, or you set up systems that help you deliver the same exceptional experience to every client, every time they come in.

The more systems you have in place, the easier it is to deliver your service consistently. Some people are afraid this will put an end to client-stylist personal chit-chat and relationship-building. I certainly don't want to take that out, but you need to be aware of the time it takes up, and the best way of doing that is to give it a place in your system.

Your 'Game Face'

Another issue is letting personal life (good or bad) creep into your work, because you run the risk of the client relationship being about you, which is not why they came into the salon. I always talk about the 'Game Face'. If you were a construction worker you would put on a hard hat because it protects you. In the hair and beauty industry, the 'Game Face' is what you put on for protection in just the same way.

While you are wearing your 'Game Face' you are thinking about your clients and not yourself. Set up triggers that remind you to put it on: it might be triggered when you put on your apron, uniform, or name badge, or you might just develop the habit of putting it on as soon as you walk into the salon. Develop a little routine that helps you get your mind off your own life, and into salon mentality. Think of the salon you work in like a stage – it's your place to perform and put in the high-energy effort that leads to a high average dollar sale.

No System = No Sales

One salon introduced some strip lashes: the ones that clients put on themselves. The day I came in, all the staff were wearing the lashes and they looked very elegant. The lashes came in a little pouch and the stock sat on the reception desk. They were great gift ideas – even the older clients could give them to their grand-daughters – and the salon sold about 15 sets per week (at $29.95 each).

It was highly profitable. But three weeks later the girls were tired of talking about lashes, and the lash sales dropped off completely because there was no system. From the salon point of view this resulted in less income, but even more importantly the clients who came in after the novelty had worn off didn't get the opportunity to learn about how great these lashes were, and decide if they wanted to purchase them or not.

How this works in practice

This means that everyone who works in your salon knows the standards. Such as:

- If someone rocks up hung-over, wearing yesterday's clothes, it's right there in black and white on the lunch room wall... Send him/her home now!
- If someone is late, it's right there on the back wall, and you can give that person a written warning immediately.
- We never discount – *ever*!

All of these standards are aimed at showing just one thing: clients come first. So we need to be ready for them, and every client is just as important as any other client. It's not just a random preference.

What this means is that when anyone walks in the door, everyone looks up and smiles. Then someone walks over and says "Hi, my name is ... How can I help you today?" or "Hi Susan, how are you?" and tells her where to sit.

It means that every person in the salon knows 'The Salon Way' of washing hair, talking points and so on, and that every client gets the same experience whether their hair is washed by the junior or the salon owner, and they always know what to expect.

> To sum up...
> How do you develop systems?
>
> I'd bet that you have a clear picture of what you'd really like to happen when people walk into your salon, and how you'd like them to feel when they walk out. Jot that down.
>
> Make a list of all the things you constantly have to talk to your team about: appearance, punctuality, greeting customers, up-sells, chatting to friends and relatives…
>
> Then think about what you want those things to look like – and write them down.

3

Make a list of all the processes you do in your salon: hair washing, scalp massage, colouring, cutting, foils, waxing, eye-brows, facials...

Then list exactly how long each process should take and what steps are involved.

What might be some relevant talking points during each process?

Talk to your staff and get their input.

Write down all these steps and tweak them until you've got a clear picture of exactly what creates a 'Wow!' response in your clients.

Now make sure that is what happens every time.

The good news is that you can start introducing systems tomorrow and tweak them as you go along. Once you have a clear working system in place, it's easy to keep using them forever.

For more information and resources head to salonsmarts.work

four

4

Setting goals that lead to satisfaction

4

You hear a lot about goals, and maybe you think they're depressing, stressful or just plain annoying. But I'd like to show you why they are essential to your success, and help you make goals to take you where you want to go.

You must have a goal! If you don't have a goal you will just continue doing what you're doing, because without a real target it's difficult to know where to aim. If you are not a goal setter, then I suggest you learn how to set effective goals as soon as possible.

When I meet with a prospective client (usually in a café), the first things I ask are "What plans do you have?" and "What are your goals?" I usually get answers like "I want to make more money" or "I want more time off."

At this point I do a little exercise to prove that this is just too loose and sloppy.

I pick up a sugar sachet and say "Throw this." That's the only instruction I give them.

Some just throw it anywhere. Others ask me "Where do you want me to throw it?" Other people think I am on drugs, or they look around for the hidden camera.

4

The ones who ask me where to throw the sachet are the ones I'm most interested in working with, because I can see that this person wants to be led, to be told what to do, but will probably ask questions and analyse along the way. I know I can really help them.

Those who just throw the sugar sachet into mid air, it tells me that they are keen to get going and will do whatever I ask them to do. It may be a little concerning that they are so trusting, or so desperate. Sometimes that's simply because they're exhausted and just want to get to the greener grass as soon as possible.

Anyway, after they throw it I say "OK, that's not exactly what I wanted." And I ask them to throw it again, but this time aiming for a pot plant. It may take a few tries, but after a while they hit the target.

The point is, you need to know exactly what you're aiming for. Then just keep at it until you do hit your target.

So, how do you set an effective goal?

You may have heard of SMART Goals, but you may never have appreciated just how clever they are.

A SMART Goal is:

S – specific
M – measurable
A – achievable
R – realistic
T – timely

Let's do a test

My goal: "I am going to sell 6 products."

I can make it more specific by saying "I am going to sell 6 products from the 'O So Soft' skin range."

Measurable? Yes, '6' is measurable.

Achievable? Yes, I think so.

Realistic? Yes, I think so.

Timely? No. I haven't said when I am going to sell them. "Today" would work. "Before lunch today" is even better.

Now my goal is much stronger: "Today I am going to sell 6 products from the 'O So Soft' skin range before lunch."

This is how you can test whether your goal is a SMART one.

How this works in practice

It's quite a lot more work to create SMART Goals than just putting down vague general goals. But it's also a lot easier to work out how to achieve them. The most successful people I know are able to visualise exactly what they want out of their business, then set about making it happen.

Maybe you want to beat your best week ever – how are you measuring that? Takings? Profits? Number of clients?

Perhaps you want your rebooking rate to be over 90%. That means 9 out of every 10 clients will make a commitment to return before they leave the salon.

Maybe you want to have one Saturday off a month, to stay in your PJs all day or do whatever you want, without being called up every 20 minutes to handle a salon issue.

Goals belong to you. They are your wishes for the future and only you can make them a reality. So they need to be sharp and pointy, not sloppy.

The simplest way to explain this is to use weight loss as an example – because I think most of us at some stage have wanted to lose a kilo (or four).

If I say "This year I hope to lose a bit of weight." OR "In the next three months I'm going to lose 6kgs at a rate of 2kg per month."

Which goal is more likely to be achieved?

The first statement isn't really a goal at all. The second statement is a realistic, measurable goal of losing 500g per week.

If I go on to add "I'm going to do that by walking every day, ordering 'Lite and Easy' meals and only drinking alcohol at the weekend."

"My sister's wedding is in four months, and I have a fabulous red dress that I will be able to wear when I am 6kgs lighter. I now weigh 67kg, so in 3 months I will weigh 61kgs."

The more refined your goal is, the more likely it is to succeed and the easier it will be to tell people about it. The more people you share your goal with, the higher the likelihood of your success.

If you are very sure it's going to happen, because you have a clear plan for achieving it, then you will be fine with telling others. But if you are just hoping you are going to succeed, you will probably keep this to yourself.

> *"The more refined your goal, the more likely it is to succeed."*

I test out someone's plan or goal by using the SMART checklist.

It will let you know if you have covered it all.

That was an example of a personal goal, but you need to have business goals, and you need to make sure everyone on your team has goals, and a plan for reaching them.

To sum up...
Set your goals and keep them visible

What I suggest you do, is to jot down all the goals you need, use the SMART checklist to define them, then stick them up where you will see them often. That way you will always know where you should focus next.

It really helps if you can see your goals at a glance. They need to pop out at you. Symbols and pictures are powerful means of visualisation, so if you have symbols and pictures for your goals, they too will be extremely powerful! One glance and the image pops into your head. That's what I want your goals to be like – very clear pictures of what it is you're after, which remind you exactly what you're aiming for. Post them wherever they are going to remind you of what you are aiming for, or what you need to accomplish.

For example, you might want to collect the kids from school every day. So, draw a clock next to a photo of the kids in their uniforms:

Kids + clock = work life balance

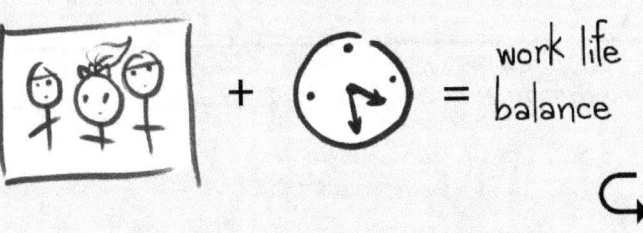

Beside your coffee machine at the salon you might have something which illustrates 'listening is everything', reminding you that your goal is to listen for clues on solving clients' concerns. This will increase your retail sales and help you reach your goal of selling 15 products per week.

Have some fun with it! Once you get the hang of it, there will be no stopping you.

'Now Goals' and 'Later Goals'

You can start by jotting down all the things you want, both large and small. Maybe you'd like to own three salons – that would be a 'Later Goal'. But you'll need to plan the steps toward it, so a 'Now Goal' might be to get the salon you already own running like a well-oiled machine.

You may not have thought about goals as a tool for helping you achieve what you want – they may seem more like something other people impose on you – but that has to change. SMART Goals can transform your life and your business.

For more information and resources head to salonsmarts.work

five

Leading your team to success

The Salon Owner is the Leader! A leader sets the tone of the salon and pretty much determines what happens. So your biggest problem is... YOU!

But that means the solution is right there in the mirror

– YOU!

YOU are the problem! *YOU* are also the solution!

If you are prepared to look at everything you do, and how you think, with a fresh set of eyes, you can turn your business into whatever you want it to be. Understanding that the problem isn't your team can be a hard pill to swallow. However, it's also exciting, because it means that you have control over your earning capacity and your future.

5

The reason why you are struggling to make the money you deserve is that you don't know what you don't know – and that's OK. Once you realise this, you can start to learn what it is you don't know.

When I am assessing a new salon (which is the first stage of my mentoring process), and I am looking over the data that tells me what's going on, I often notice that two therapists/stylists are working side-by-side yet getting very different results.

They have the same:

- place to work: same chairs, mirrors and treatment rooms
- street, neighbourhood and town
- products, tools and equipment to work with
- opportunities

Only one thing sets them apart, and it's that one girl has a steady stream of A and B grade clients with the odd C grade client; while the other seems to get mostly C grade clients, with a few Bs – and every D grade client in the district! (Learn more about grading clients in Chapter 16 *Unhappy clients, bad clients and common mistakes*). Is that just bad luck?

Clearly, one girl has built a great clientele for herself, has heaps of requests and gets all the happy customers, while the girl right beside her hasn't and doesn't. If you ask the second girl about her clientele, she goes straight into excuse-mode:

- Parking issues
- She hasn't been there long enough yet

- People don't want to spend money on luxuries because of taxes and the rising cost of living
- They buy products on eBay

… and 101 other reasons why she gets all the dodgy clients. Same opportunities, yet one succeeds while the other struggles.

So, this is what I think. It's the same with salon owners – the problem and the solution start with you. You can either get results, or get reasons why you don't have results. It's exciting because it puts you in the driver's seat: you can change your thinking, and that can change your life.

5 *Were you trained to lead?*

I wasn't. And most salon owners I meet weren't either. We get frustrated. We don't understand why we aren't making good money. We are working hard enough, but we don't know how to get the team to perform. Clients that we are sure we looked after just disappear without even saying goodbye. I call this the 'Shoot me now!' feeling.

But maybe this isn't your fault. Have you ever learned these skills? Maybe you've been to a seminar (or three!) and left feeling excited about the changes you need to make. Then, heading back to the salon all ready to get on with your plan, you find that someone has gone home sick, or the phone (which rang while you were still in the car) has a client on the other end bitching about how she was overcharged yesterday… Like I said "Shoot me now!"

Now you feel even worse. "Shit, shit, shit!" If you haven't been taught how to be a business owner, then don't be so hard on yourself. Give your accountant a pair of scissors and ask him to do a haircut – just make sure you aren't the recipient. He can't do it, so don't beat yourself up about not being able to do his job. You need to make a plan, learn what needs to be done (maybe get some help so you can actually learn it now) – then keep doing it forever. That's the way to turn your business around.

This is where I think regular coaching is more valuable than a single seminar: you get measurable baby steps and some serious checking-in on a regular basis. The best decision I ever made was to start working with a Business Coach: someone who helped me learn what I needed to learn and do what I needed to do; someone who checked in with me regularly and kicked my bum if needed to make sure I took whatever action we'd agreed upon.

One of my clients came to me because his salon wasn't making the money he needed. He was doing the 'cha cha' with his salon, taking one step forward and one step back. He had a team of five or six and one of them was a little hard to handle, so he avoided her. He didn't like her so he avoided talking to her, and he didn't hold staff meetings because he didn't want anything to do with her. Ironically, she was his most profitable team member, while the team member whom he liked the most was actually costing him money.

So we started to explore what was going on. I helped him to see that:

- This is a business, not a friendship group.
- Avoiding her was not a solution on any planet, especially not on planet Earth.
- The only way forward was to have team meetings as well as one-on-one meetings.

I thought he was going to be sick, he went so pale! So I promised that I would conduct a meeting that would engage the team, and that at no point was it ever going to be uncomfortable. He said he'd rather streak at the local football Grand Final! But seeing as what he was doing was obviously not working, he agreed.

> **The problem and solution start with you.**

So I started running the team meetings with him. We made them short and we certainly made them fun. It changed the way the team thought about meetings and they were happy to attend. In fact, when he was going away and suggested they skip the meetings, the team felt it was such an essential part of keeping the energy flowing one of the girls took over for him.

Talk about a turnaround! When you have a strong culture it means your salon works whether you are there or not.

After hearing this from his team, the salon owner rang to tell me about their conversation and concluded with "The problem wasn't them, it was me. You knew that didn't you?" I just grinned.

What I really love about what I do is that I don't hand you a fish that will feed you for a single day. I get you a fishing rod, a reel, some fishing line, some bait, and then I show you where to find lots of fish, so you can feed yourself forever.

So, how do you lead your team to success?

If you own a salon and you want it to be successful, then you need to be a leader, and that means you have to be the best possible version of yourself. That also means you need to work harder on yourself than on anyone else because your success, your confidence, your knowledge and your direction is contagious. People will be drawn to you. Your team will want to stay around you because you're always looking for the next exciting chapter, but that means that you need to make some decisions.

First things first. Is running a salon what you really want to do? Maybe it's not your gig after all. Decide if you can, or even want to do this. You absolutely need to decide to jump in or get out – you can't sit on the fence! Because everything you do will be watched – and I do mean everything. If you say "No, this is not what I want", that's OK. Now you know, and you can make an exit plan. Really look inside for your answer, and take your time to work out exactly what you want. Then agree that you are the problem and also that you are the solution, so you have all the control over what happens next. That's the bit that excites me – because if you work for someone else you don't have that control.

Now let's look at your team. They're not going to 'get it' the same way you do because they don't have the same level of control. Their own life is more important to them than your business is. Oops. So you can't expect from them the same level of passion and initiative you have. This is probably the #1 frustration I hear from salon owners. Sometimes you just want to scream "For God's sake, are you thick or something? Even blind Freddy can see what's going on!"

The fact is, most of the time your team have no idea that what it is they do that drives you mad. Not only aren't they thinking about how they annoy you, they aren't thinking at all – and that's your problem. For example, they call in sick when you know that they are not that sick. There is no way that you would call in sick with that degree of illness, yet you can't say anything because it will come across as though you just don't care about them.

There's a good reason why they are employees and you own the place: they like the privileges that being an employee brings. They are happy to leave the responsibility and commitment to you, and just 'do their part'. You gave that luxury up when you bought your salon, because the bigger picture was more appealing. You had a vision to build a great place to work, and it was going to be even more awesome because it would be your kingdom and you would be making all the decisions! What you didn't factor in were other people who don't share your drive or passion, who just don't get it.

The worst part is that often you pay them more then you pay yourself. So it doesn't matter whether you had a profitable week or a terrible week, they still get paid. Yet your income is directly affected by the performance of the salon. That is enough to frustrate (or excite) anyone.

Your team members are entitled to privileges that you are no longer entitled to. However, if your business becomes a huge success, then the benefits will far outweigh those relatively few privileges of being on a wage. I suggest you read Chapter 10 *Knowing exactly how much money you need to break even.*

The road to becoming a successful salon owner is simple – just two choices:

1. Step up and take on the responsibility for everything.
2. Step back and delegate.

Most salon owners go for the first option, but not enough of you make the second choice. You try stepping back, to test it, but more often than not your team let you down. So you go back to role of doing everything, and that's where you stay.

You have to learn the art of delegation, because that's at the heart of leadership. Leaders are only 5% of the population and I think 3% of those 5% aren't natural leaders; they had to learn it or at least perfect it. Think about who you would go to right now if you had a problem that you couldn't solve by yourself – a person who could lead you to the answer. I'd bet you can't think of more than five people who could help you. Take out your parents and you'll definitely have less than five – that's because leaders and problem solvers are rare. But you can learn to be that person for your team.

If you are a strong leader and you have the answers, your team will want to please you, and they'll want to stay around because you make their lives easier. You can make sense of what's going on and they will be drawn to you. The reason you own a salon is because you are brave: you were willing to put your heart and soul into your vision and make a plan. You may not have realised it at the time, but you put your hand up to be a leader. Your team didn't do that – or at least they haven't yet – and you need to accept that.

How this works in practice

We had a very clear leave policy and I can remember as though it were yesterday the time a staff member asked me for two days off. It was a couple of months ahead, she had filled in the paper work and she was asking for a Wednesday and Thursday off. I thought it was very considerate of her and I was pleased she hadn't asked for Friday and Saturday off, so I told her to put the dates into the computer. It wasn't until weeks later that I noticed she had chosen the two days leading up to Easter – so she ended up with 10 days straight. (Her family lived in Queensland and she saw it as a great opportunity to go home and see them.) Easter means the salon is closed Friday and Saturday, so the two days leading up are probably the two busiest days of the year, apart from Christmas. I felt like she had tricked me and I was really annoyed.

She hadn't broken any law; she'd just failed to mention that it wasn't just any old Wednesday and Thursday. I took it personally because that's what I used to do. It took me a while to realise there's no point taking these things personally. She was well within the guidelines and it's not her business – it's mine! To be really truthful, I was a little jealous that she had more choices than I did.

I call my solution 'double white lines' because it's like lines on the road: nobody crosses over the double white lines because it's not an option. We have some boundaries in the salon that no-one crosses – NOT EVER! I've decided what those boundaries are, and no-one else needs to think about them. The normal line in the middle of the road is broken because it gives us options. You don't want your team to have to make decisions all day. If they have to think about too many things they're wasting a lot of energy. So, if we put 'double white lines' around the things we don't want them to wonder about, suddenly they'll have lots of energy freed up to make creative decisions about things they are responsible for – like clients. It saves a lot of guessing and negotiating.

5

OR

To sum up...
How can you lead your team better?

To run any business you must be a leader. That means people like you and I need to lead. Maybe you're not a natural leader, but if you work at it anyone can learn to lead.

As a leader you need a vision of where you want to go, and a picture of how that looks like in practice.

Then, you need to accept that your team will never have the same level of passion as you do. That's OK, because the ones who do come along brimming with drive and vision are born leaders who will want their own salon just like you, and they will move on.

Remember that no-one drives to work thinking "How can I give my boss the shits today?"

Also remember that any solution that solves your problem is a great solution, so don't be too precious about it.

If you avoid doing things because you don't like doing them, they don't go away. In my experience they will just get bigger and bigger. That problem will always be there to annoy you.

> So, whatever it is that you don't like, challenge yourself to change the way you think about it. Look at it from another angle. What's the risk if you don't solve it? What's the reward if you do?
>
> Didn't you start your salon so that you could be in charge and make all the decisions? So take charge. Take charge of yourself, your team and your salon.

For more information and resources head to salonsmarts.work

six

6

Building, nurturing and motivating your team

I want to cover a few team management basics in this chapter, because I think we all know deep down that everyone in the salon needs to work together as a team – we're not just a group of individuals. It's a common problem I see in the hair and beauty industry. Often it's because we're all busy doing our part of the mix and not thinking about anyone else, but also because of an ancient Roman disease called Interruptus Continuus (In-ter-rup-tus Con-tin-you-us) which is rampant in all our salons. Interruptus Continuus is that terrible condition where you are always either being interrupted, just about to be interrupted, or trying to determine where you were up to before you were interrupted. It's a dangerous disease that threatens your productivity – and your sanity – and it's an epidemic in our industry!

If we don't make time to talk, it won't happen. The reality is that you're lucky to get more than 2 minutes with even one of your team members in the course of a normal day, let alone the whole group.

My essential tools for building, nurturing and motivating your team are:

- Team meetings
- One-on-one meetings
- Pat-Smack-Pat

If you use these tools, I can just about guarantee you will learn some things about yourself and your team that will transform your salon from a burden to a joy, because you'll have a team of people who are pulling together to achieve both your goals for the salon and their own goals. In some salons you might have certain staff who won't work as part of a team, so this gives you the chance to recognise them and gently help them to see they don't belong.

So, how do you build, nurture and motivate your team?

You might be thinking "Interruptus Continuus is not really a problem in my salon." Are you sure? In a hair salon, you'll be taking a call from the lady who is telling you how to cut her 14 year old son's hair that afternoon, and that she will pay when she comes in to pick him up. Then you'll be checking if your client is happy to have Susie put her colour on, and Sarah is asking if she can open another tester of wax, and the door opens and you need to move your car because the lady from the café is going home early and can't get out. And so it goes on. Never a dull moment, and never time to collect your thoughts and have a real conversation.

In beauty it's even worse! Your team disappear like gynaecologists on roller skates when you try to catch them between treatment rooms. They come out of their room and you start to say something important, then the client appears from nowhere and you have to wait.

Sound familiar? That's why you need to plan meetings with your team, and with the individuals you work with. They help us keep on track, and give us time to talk.

Team meetings that add buzz!

In the previous chapter, *Leading your team to success*, I talked about the team meeting. It doesn't need to be long and serious – in fact, I suggest you keep it fun, focused and close to 15 minutes in length. It needs to have a structure and a point, and you need to put some thought into what you can get through in the time. It's really a time when you share your goals with the team and you all brainstorm ways to achieve them, and the numbers that will take the salon in the right direction.

Often someone will say to me "But what can the girl who does facials and the ones who do waxing, nails or hair say to help each other?" I usually hear this in salons with 5-10 employees who provide a wide range of hair and beauty treatments, and I usually put a bit of humour into my answer. The reality is that every client has an entire body that your colleagues could treat – if your specialty is facials then why not mention the latest nail treatment, or hair treatment. Perhaps there's a makeup artist in the salon and you learn that your client is having the facial a few days prior to a special event so you could suggest a professional make-up for the occasion, or having her hair done.

> "Of course you can all help each other out, and the team meeting is the perfect place to work out how that can happen."

I mean to say... When was the last time you saw hair without a face, fingers and toenails, and a body to go with it in your salon? Of course you can all help each other out, and the team meeting is the perfect place to work out how that can happen.

One-on-ones that add snap!

They don't make hairdressers like they used to – I believe they shut the factory down in the 1980s. I love Gen. Y but I have to say I didn't always. I was stuck in the headspace of "Bloody hell! I have to thank you for doing your basic job – the one I pay you for!"

This new generation won't miss their lunch break and they want a pay slip every week – preferably a generous one. I have three Gen. Ys myself, so I can see the other side of the argument – and really there's no point fighting reality. I never wanted to be one of those oldies, that told you how they walked 5 miles to and from school every day and if it rained they got wet so I worked out that my only option was to learn how to communicate with them and make it work.

It was accidental, really. I had a terrible time finding seniors who wanted to keep learning. By about the age of 26 all the seniors I found were 'too old' to see that the client's satisfaction is everything. On the other hand the Gen. Ys had big ideas! Mostly airy-fairy ones that they hadn't figured out how to fund – like the one who was going to travel around the world on a yacht but who had trouble finding her car keys – but at least they had big plans and they're dreaming of more. So they were open to learn and to grow professionally, but I realised that for that to happen I needed to make time to say what I wanted to say, and plan for the improvement I was looking in my business by sharing my vision with them.

My days were jumping and my clients were back to back, so I started meeting with them one-on-one and keeping notes. In between meetings I'd jot down anything I wanted to talk about with them, and I kept notes on each member so that over time I ended up with a document that covered everything they did or said that we could use to track performance and give encouragement. It was really their opinion of where they thought they were at – in all areas of their role in the salon, not just in their skills.

From these notes I made some discoveries about what was consistently being discussed. I believe every problem you face in the salon falls into four main categories:

1. Skill
2. Attitude
3. Team
4. Neglect

I soon worked out that if I let them tell me what areas they felt they needed help in; and identify exactly how they could improve, along with when they thought it could be achieved, they owned it. It was their idea and they worked at improving (most of the time).

This doesn't mean that at times they weren't being naughty little witches and I had to show them that their behaviour wasn't going to cut it, but I usually found that asking what they were prepared to do got me the response I really wanted to hear. Along the way I got some really awesome insights like:

- I should not jump to conclusions about why they're doing this – most of them don't set out to make me mad.
- I could be more patient with my team members and provide more feedback (60% of Gen. Y want feedback on their performance from their boss, and 35% want it 2-3 times per day!)
- They need more practice and should get more models lined up so that when one cancels there are still two more.

What I was doing here was making them accountable for their own performance and when we worked through things in this way, we all learned a lot.

Fifteen minutes weekly is plenty of time for your one-on-one meeting and ideally it should be done in a café, not in the business. I called them my $3.80 insurance policy. Why? Well, usually information literally fell out of them, and more often than not I'd learn if they were planning a family, or thinking about going overseas for two months the next year. Just by sitting down over a cup of coffee with my hairdresser or beauty therapist and asking "How can I help you?" or "What are you working on?" I'd gather priceless information that would let me plan ahead.

I also discovered that they really did want to know how I felt they were going. They were looking for feedback on their efforts and they were grateful for all the opportunities they were getting. That was my experience, and my coaching clients have found the same thing too. There are some things that you don't need to deal with in team meetings because it's just one person who has the problem. One-on-one meetings mean that you don't have to waste team time on those things. In any case, if you've got a performance issue it is better to talk about it privately, so that they can tell you honestly what is holding them back. Often they don't want to be sales people. You can learn more about how I address this in Chapter 13 *The 3 'R's – Rebooking, Recommending and Retail*. It's all about honestly talking about what is holding them back so you can address it.

6

> *"15 minutes weekly is plenty of time for your one-on-one meetings – ideally in a café. I call them my $3.80 insurance policy."*

One-on-ones are like putting tap-dancing shoes on. Once the shoes are on, you just keep testing out the tap-tap-tap and before you know it you are making a hell of a noise. Once we got out of the salon our relationship shifted so by the time the offee had arrived we were knee-deep in what they thought would be a great idea. "Do you think we could get a make-up range in?" Or "Let's all go to Hair Expo as a team." Some things aren't such great ideas, and that gives you a chance to talk about 'Why not' – others are excellent. We used to have trouble pleasing everyone with the music we played in the salon. One of the girls suggested that we had a day each. She set up a roster and whoever was rostered got to choose the music for the salon for a whole day. It instantly took the whinging away.

I can't tell you how important the one-on-ones are. They are going to save you a lot of time, and they are also going to make you money, as you will soon find out if the person is interested in making improvements. They are where you get to praise their performance and get them excited about how they can go further. It's about them, not just the salon.

Motivating your team

Gen. Ys have been told how good they are from birth. Parents, teachers, sports coaches ... you name it ... they learned they could do and be anything they wanted to be and have anything they wanted before they could talk. One thing they didn't learn – how to empty a dishwasher without being asked.

You've seen those TV shows like *Australia's Got Talent?* Well, I think we had to have them. Somebody had to tell these kids "YOU CANT SING!" because Mum and Dad weren't going to. Gen. Ys love feedback – about 35% want you to give them feedback 2 to 3 times a day, but they find it extremely difficult to be told that they are not so good at something.

Well, I had a team of nine so that is a fair whack of feedback to give. What I learned is that it goes a long way to developing communication – especially when I used the Pat-Smack-Pat pattern.

> " *Be authentic, vulnerable, transparent and clear with them, and they will love and respect you for it.* "

Pat means to praise. *Smack* means to point out the areas they're falling short in – the ones they need to change. Then *Pat* again. If you wrap any critique between two praises, you will be amazed at the positive outcome. I tried to keep my proportions pretty much ⅓ Praise, ⅓ Critique, ⅓ Praise – like I said, Gen. Ys like feedback, but they're used to praise.

On the other hand, when I'm working with someone who is very timid, and lacks confidence, I'll beef up the praise and cut the critique back. You need to build up your relationship before you lay on too much heavy criticism. Once you've established a strong relationship, the team member knows you are invested in **their** development and not just being mean.

You might be saying "Dear me, how soft this generation is!" That's the reality we're working with, so my solution is to learn to speak their language – because I'm the one with most to lose if this doesn't work out. Kids today have more choices than we ever did, and they are not scared to stand up for what they believe in. Be a part of their dreams and you will be surprised how far you go.

Firm works well, some things are negotiable and others are not. Be authentic, vulnerable, transparent, and clear with them and they will love and respect you for it.

My father used to ask one of us to clean his shoes every Saturday. He was a bookmaker and needed them polished before he went to the races. I can remember taking them to him, feeling quite pleased with my effort, and he took one look and said "You missed the rims." So I went back and applied more polish to the rims. It never occurred to me that perhaps he could have said "Thank you, they look fabulous for a first try, but I would like it if you could put a little more polish on this bit here, because I stand up on a platform and it will be seen. I am sure you wouldn't have missed it if I had mentioned that in the first place. Would you do that little bit again for me please?" But that's what today's kids are used to.

The Naked Salon

If you are always giving praise and someone really mucks up, you are in a good position to come down hard on him or her. Only praise if it's deserved. If you can't find something to praise a person about, then maybe that person needs to work elsewhere. You are not responsible for sorting out every person's problems – you have a salon to run!

A quick word about critique

Sarcasm is not critique – and it usually backfires. I was meeting with a salon owner and she was setting up a few things, so we could leave to have our meeting when her team member came in – late. The owner looked at her watch and sarcastically said "Good afternoon." It was 9.02 am.

I thought "What good could possibly come from this sarcastic remark?" So toward the end of our meeting I asked her about it, and she replied "She does this all the time."

I offered her a suggestion (after all, that's why we were meeting). Next time she comes in late and goes through to the back room, just excuse yourself from your client and say to her "I see that you are late again and before you leave tonight I would like to have a chat about it." That would take you 60 seconds, tops – and then go back to your client.

When you are having your one-on-one, point out that she is always well dressed and well presented and clearly loves the industry, however you can't have her coming late and keeping clients waiting for her. It's the wrong way round. Then let her give you all the reasons why she's late. At the end of that, you can say "I'm happy to give you a few tips on getting ready the night before, but you need to do whatever it takes to be here on time." Then follow it up with some more praise about her dedication and passion and remind her that the hair and beauty business is all about wowing clients, and being on time is really important.

She tried it, and you know what? Her problem team member changed. Sarcasm didn't work, but taking time to talk it through did! Pat-Smack-Pat.

If you keep doing things the same way, then the results will be the same. When I started using Pat-Smack-Pat, not only did the atmosphere in my salon improve, I also went from not being able to find staff to having people randomly drop off their CVs in case I had an opening. That is an awesome place to be. What you focus on grows and what you need to do is put 'sunshine and water' onto the seeds that you plant. By that I mean praise people for what they do well. If you praise people twice as much as you critique them, things will change for the better.

Just for fun!

Now and then – just for fun – or when we are introducing a new product, I buy six different chocolate bars and put them in a bowl under the counter. I say to the team "The first one to make a product sale today gets first pick and, yes, if you sell three products you can have three chocolate bars."

It transforms an ordinary day into a fun day and engages the team in some friendly competition. You won't believe how much of an incentive a chocolate bar can be yet it has only cost you a few dollars. You'll find them bragging about who got the Mars Bar and who got left with the Turkish Delight. In the meantime, they've upped your retail sales and built a stronger team spirit.

> To sum up...
>
> What do you really need to do to make this work?
>
> Maybe you're thinking this sounds like you'll have to waste a whole lot of time in meetings. There are two problems with this attitude:
>
> 1. It stinks! and
>
> 2. It will transform your outcomes.
>
> Listen, if you can't face a 15 minute team meeting with your whole team and 15 minutes with each member every week in order to achieve your goals for the salon, then maybe you should sell or close your salon. That's all it takes. If you have 10 team members you'll be done in less than 3 hours – and you don't need to schedule them back-to-back either.

Here are a few tips to make your meetings efficient and productive:

Schedule them weekly: give everyone a time slot and don't move them around.

1. Keep notes for each person so you know what you want to talk about and make an agenda for your team meeting.
2. Use Pat-Smack-Pat when you have criticisms to make.
3. Focus on salon goals and individual goals – maybe a team member wants to learn a new skill – that is good for your salon as well as the individual.

Research indicates that Gen. Ys love feedback 2-3 times per day. You can use that to your advantage by giving them enough positive feedback to make them feel valued, and sandwiching in the critique they need to improve. You'll be astounded at the difference that makes in your results.

For more information and resources head to salonsmarts.work

OR

seven

Mystery shoppers, quality control and confidence

When was the last time you went into a salon and had a facial or a hair cut and paid full whack? When I ask this question it's quite common to hear that the last time was before the person actually started in the industry. Beauty professionals maybe not so much, because there are new treatments coming out all the time and so you're a bit more experimental, but hairdressers almost always have someone on the team do their hair after work. Since you rarely pay full price for what you sell, you lose sight of what it feels like to be a client. It's really dangerous to sell something you never buy yourself.

When I am doing group training and ask this question, I might get one person (or two at the most) say they had a blow wave or something similar because they were away somewhere and had a wedding to attend. In other words, they were forced to.

The sentence usually finishes with "and it wasn't great", followed by the tale about how they fixed it when they got home. It's a bit like the 'vegetarian who works in the butcher shop' (not that this would ever happen because vegetarians have a very strong belief system) – but the point is, they may 'know' about the meat, but they never experience it. Our industry has the same problem: we don't really understand the customer's experience because we don't ever experience it.

So, I suggest that you find out what it's like to be a client and that you also get some 'mystery shoppers' to come into your business. I used to have them all the time and the girls in the salon used to take pride in guessing who they were. When I still owned a salon I would give my coaching clients a free service in my salon so that they could see what I meant. Mostly things went well, but sometimes the girls missed important things and we all learned from it: the good and the not-so-good.

When was the last time you had your own work critiqued? By that I mean when was the last time somebody actually evaluated the work you produce? If you can't remember, it's been too long! You don't have to make it difficult – you could simply have your haircut checked by another team member. Just because you were good at it 25 years ago, does not mean that you are still good at it today – and even if you are the best cutter in the salon, others can still give you helpful feedback (or praise!).

My mother Moira is 86. She had nine children: five sons and four daughters. When we were growing up, Mum cooked breakfast, lunch and dinner, and she could make one kilogram of minced steak easily feed a dozen people. She had the ability to stretch food to suit the crowd, and my father Maurie seemed to have a knack of adding one extra mouth to feed right on the bell. Mum was by no means a fancy cook, but she repeated our favourite dishes without a recipe and they were exactly the same: always delicious and just the way my father liked them.

Mum now lives on a horse stud in a house about 100m away from my sister Pauline and her husband Peter. Mum likes to help out where she can, so she irons sometimes and most weeks she used to make a casserole for Pauline and Peter. At 86, Mum's cooking isn't like it used to be, and Pauline and Peter didn't really like casseroles. However, every week Mum made a casserole for Pauline and every week Pauline gave it to her Golden Retriever Yabba. As anyone with a Golden Retriever knows, they eat everything! The casserole dish went through the dishwasher and back over to Mum's. Everyone was happy.

Until one day, very suddenly Yabba was gone. This was very sad, and Mum decided to make a casserole so Pauline wouldn't have to cook while she was grieving for her best friend. My mother would rather live on a piece of cake with a cup of tea. She just orders dessert when you take her out for dinner, and insists that at 86 she can do whatever she wants. When you mention her diet, she grins and says that sugar is a preservative too. So, it's a long time since she's actually eaten her own casseroles.

This particular afternoon my sister invited my mother to stay for dinner. She opens the fridge and there wasn't much to choose from – just the casserole (because Yabba wasn't around to eat it). So Pauline warmed it up, served it, and handed a plate to my mother. My mother took one mouthful and said "I can't eat this! Dear me, it's terrible! I don't think I should cook any more." (And that was that!. My dear mother, who never over-thinks anything, hasn't cooked a casserole since.) So my sister just smiled and got them both an egg on toast.

Like I say – just because you were fantastic 10 years ago, or even 5 years ago doesn't mean you still are. Get some feedback.

So, when was the last time you got honest feedback?

I'd like you to think about the last time you had outside critique of your business. It's a scary idea isn't it? Inviting someone to take a close look at what you do and give you honest feedback. In the restaurant industry, there are regular food critics that show up at random. Without warning! And then they write up an article and tell the world exactly what they think.

I would love this to be as common in the hair and beauty industry because it would be something to strive for. But they only see a small slice of your salon, so their critique might not be the truth. Well, so do your clients, and their perception of your business is their truth. We have to get to a place in which the standard of service is so consistent there is no argument about it – and that is the challenge!

My experience tells me that as the owner of the salon, you are probably the most skilled person in your team and therefore here lies another challenge. Who do you invite to critique you, while you are also doing most of the work, running the business and training the juniors?

There are many ways to keep on top of this, but you need to make a plan for doing so. Go to industry nights, product launches, catwalks, 'Look and Learn' workshops, hands-on workshops, guest speakers – you just need to get out there and be amongst like-minded people.

> *Someone needs to control the quality and that person needs to be you.*

What I find interesting about salons is that it's not until a staff member leaves and you find yourself looking after their clients and thinking "This is not good! Why hasn't this client been offered this treatment or that one?" Or you see that the work quality is terrible. Now you are feeling terrible about the quality of work that has left your salon, and so you should. Reputation is everything!

Next you start wondering about those other clients that are missing, and you lie awake wondering where Mrs Jones has gone, and where Natasha is getting her hair done. Trust me, if you don't have a system that allows you to identify your lost clients on a weekly basis you are definitely working hard but not smart.

Someone needs to control the quality and that person needs to be you – the owner.

Clients aren't always picky about quality. The number one reason a client leaves you is because they feel they were taken for granted. That is really sad, because loyalty is rare today and it is far more expensive and time-consuming to find a new client than it is to keep an existing one happy. That means you need to take a good look at your returning client data every week, and find out who looked after them last. This is one of my favourite coaching tricks, because the clients I work with are almost always shocked at two things:

1. Some members of your team lose more clients than others.
2. There are more lost clients than they ever imagined.

Most computer software today can go back 16 weeks. If a client has not been back to you in four months they have probably chosen someone else. So, if you're not looking back 16 weeks and finding who has gone and trying to discover why, you really are asking for trouble. You may realise that there are certain members of your team who are losing clients steadily.

If that's the case, it's your responsibility to find out why, and deal with the problem. Most of the time it's just a question of training and advice and you can deal with it in the weekly one-on-one session with each team member.

Working smarter is always my goal, and this is one of the many things that I believe will set you on your way. Deal with the facts. The numbers don't lie.

As funny as the story about my mother's horrible casserole is, your clients aren't related to you and they won't continue to pay for something they are not happy with. On the other hand, if you're keeping on top of things, getting good feedback and working on problem areas, you can be almost certain your numbers will reflect that growth.

> **To sum up...**
> **How do you get feedback, and what should you do with it?**
>
> You need to make opportunities to get feedback on your own skills and your salon.
>
> You need to give feedback to members of your team.
>
> Arrange a 'mystery shopper' swap with other salons to get feedback.
>
> Check the numbers in your software and see what they tell you.

> Feedback is just as likely to be positive as negative. So you may learn some areas where you need to improve, but you also get to feel good about the things that are already great. That applies to your salon as a whole, and the individuals in it.
>
> The only problems that can't be solved are the ones you ignore and just hope will go away. So add some 'water and sunshine' to the things you want to grow, and do some pruning on the areas that aren't going so well.

For more information and resources head to salonsmarts.work

7

The Naked Salon

eight

8

Setting expectations and training your team

If you ask anyone who owns a business what their biggest challenge is, they will tell you it's getting the right people. It's no different in salons: any salon owner will tell you their biggest challenge is building the right team. Without a team you've really just bought yourself a job. With a team, even if it's just two of you, you are well on your way to having a business.

Develop a strong, consistent team and you'll have a strong, consistent business. On the other hand, if your team is constantly changing, so is your bottom line. The only way you can judge whether your hair and beauty business is achieving your goals, is if it makes money whether you are there or not. This will only happen when you have a solid team!

So, you really can't settle for less than the best you can do in this area of team building.

I often ask salon owners to tell me about their best employee. They smile as they list all the qualities that make them great. Then I ask about their worst employee. They're not smiling as they run through all the qualities they hate. So I say "Imagine if every person on your team were like your best employee" and they say how great that would be. Then I ask them "What if they were all like your worst team member?" They reply "I would be pulling my hair out." So then I ask "You're OK with pulling *some* of your hair out – just not all of it?"

I do this because if you have the skill to find some great team members, yet still allow average or below average employees to be in your team, it doesn't make any sense at all. Why would you do this? You don't really think that finding a good employee is just luck, do you?

A lot of salon owners make decisions based on feelings. I know that our industry is a 'feel good' industry – but business is no place for emotionally driven decisions. There is no area where it's more important to make decisions based on the facts than the area of team members. We get to know too much about them, and that makes it almost impossible to make a decision just on the facts. But get this straight – Your team is *not* your family, and they're *not* your friends – they are your **Valued Employees!**

It's like the 'chummy mummy' – a modern term for someone who is being a friend to their child instead of a mother. A mother is a far more important role and you dilute it when you make it casual like this. Children have lots of friends, but they usually only have one mother. The same is true for salons. Being friends with your staff dilutes the important role you have. You are their support and their mentor, but not their friend. They have plenty of friends, but only one boss (at any time).

Your business is your livelihood, your children's future, and your superannuation: it determines how well you live now, and how secure your future is. Your business income directly decides whether you'll holiday in a tent or a five star hotel. (It's different if you can afford five stars and choose the tent. I sleep under the stars whenever I can – the indoor hotel variety, that is, not the outdoor natural ones. If I can't plug something in to a power point, I don't want to stay there.)

So why would you allow somebody into your business who isn't suitable – and if they do get in, why would you let them stay? If you let this happen, you greatly risk your chances of success. Do you really want to settle for mediocrity? Often I talk to salon owners who are happy if they can pay their bills on time. You don't need to settle for that! You must strive to have the best salon ever and that means you need the best team ever.

Any time you allow someone in who is 'just average' to stay around on your team, you are saying to the others that "near enough is good enough". Don't do that! When you strive for the best you will stop rocking back and forth like Nanna's rocking chair and start going places.

Lots of us start with a team of one and we grow it slowly, one person at a time. I often say that employees are like husbands: it's better to collect them one at a time – and if you can collect a good husband (or boyfriend), you can find good staff too. There are good people around if you open your eyes and start looking.

If you have a team of two and you get a phone call to say a team member is unwell, you've just lost 50% of your team in one phone call. If you have five on your team and one calls in sick, you only lose 20% of your team, and the other four can quickly absorb that person's work for the day. This kind of safety really only comes once you have five or more on your team, but it's worth aiming at. Getting to this place can seem really difficult, but if you start adding them 'one at a time' you can do it. Then you'll have that awesome feeling that everything is going to be fine.

So, do you really need to be tough on your team?

"Yes!"

The hair and beauty industry is full of polite niceness. We often find it difficult to say what we need or want from a team

team member and we never plan to move someone on. Now, I don't think moving them on should be your first strategy for dealing with a problem staff member (See Chapter 5 *Leading your team to success* and Chapter 6 *Building, nurturing and motivating your team*), but it often surprises me just how much salon owners tolerate. When the person finally leaves they are relieved and even happy – but they never said anything to them directly while they were working there. It's silly really, because your team represents your brand, and without a good team you will continue to struggle to have a successful business.

> *Teach people to take initiative and make decisions that are in the best interest of your clients.*

There was a salon I worked with, and they had a chap who was very likeable: happy, lots of fun, and the clients loved him. That's where the problem was. He under-performed more often than he performed; and he often undercharged clients. He was a classic example of someone who would not dream of spending that kind of money on his own hair and beauty care, and he assumed that everyone else was the same. He never recommended or up-sold unless he was in a group challenge; and then he only did it because we were watching.

I called this 'flat tyres' because I would pump up his tyres and he would improve for a few days – or even weeks. The trouble was, the minute I took my eyes off him, his tyres went flat and he stopped recommending services and selling retail. Part of the owner's role is to motivate the team. However, if a senior person in your team does not make any significant change after many opportunities, it is time for them to move elsewhere. The owner tolerated this poor performance for about two years, even though he caused trouble amongst the team and needed to be disciplined from time to time. Finally the owner had enough, took action, and the business did not suffer financially at all. The clients were delighted with the better quality service they received from others in the team.

How this works in practice

I usually start with the weakest person in the team because that is often where we can get the greatest results. This person is usually thrilled that they are getting so much attention, and they become the person you want them to be. Sometimes it doesn't work out this way, and they decide that the lazy, slack approach to working in this salon has come to an end, so they leave. That's OK, the right team members get excited and come with you on the journey, and those who don't get it, jump off. Now you need to replace this person with someone better. It's an opportunity to improve your team.

I call this the water level. If the water in your business is five inches deep, then clearly everybody can stand up, but as you improve the quality of service, the water level starts to rise. As it continues to rise, people will need to swim in your new style of business or choose to work somewhere else. It's OK either way. What I won't accept is for them to stay around and be a negative influence.

> To sum up...
> Why do you need to take your team performance seriously?
>
> Your team represents you every day on the floor. It's the most valuable asset you have in your business. I like to go into a salon where I cannot tell who the owner is. If you can tell who the owner is then it shows that the others aren't acting in the way that you want them to. When I worked in a salon I was often asked if I was the owner's wife because I had a sense of authority – which he had delegated to me in certain areas.
>
> Teach people to take initiative and make decisions that are in the best interest of your clients. It's good for your business. And don't tolerate mediocrity: it will stop your salon from being the best it can possibly be.

For more information and resources head to salonsmarts.work

nine

9

Knowing and growing your average dollar sale

There are only three things you need to manage in your salon if you want to make money:

1. **How many clients you have.** If they have an awesome experience they will tell their friends.
2. **How much they spend on your services.** If they get an awesome result they will spend more.
3. **How often they return.** If you are awesome they will be happy to come often.

Deal with these, and talking to your accountant will make you happy, not stressed.

This chapter is about increasing how much clients spend on your services: your *average dollar sale*.

Your average dollar sale needs to be awesome – and here's why: it tells you everything you need to know about what is *really* going on in the business. I was lucky enough to learn the importance of this early in my salon days. The truth is that increasing your average dollar sale is fairly easy, yet it makes an enormous difference to your profitability.

In this chapter we'll talk about the importance of the average dollar sale:

- What is it?
- What difference does it make?
- How can you improve it?

I talk about hiring and firing staff elsewhere – here we're going to look at Jake and Danielle's clients and takings in a week and work out their average dollar sale.

Jake earns $1,950 for the salon. He sees 25 clients, so his average dollar sale is $78 ($1,950/25).

Danielle's total earning for the salon is $2,950. She sees 25 clients too, but her average dollar sale is $118 ($2,950/25).

Each has the same number of clients, but Danielle earns $1,000 more for the salon than Jake does, and that makes an enormous difference to your bottom line!

There might be lots of reasons for this difference in their takings, but the core lesson is: if you're paying Jake and Danielle the same wages, Danielle is a far better investment. Right?

Now before you go off and sack Jake, let's look at why Jake's average dollar sale is so much lower, and what we can do about it – because Jake's a great guy, and his clients love him!

In my experience working with salon owners, there's always something you can do to increase your average dollar sale. Just imagine what your business would look like if each employee generated an extra $1,000 in sales per week!

I don't want to over-simplify here. There are a lot of factors that contribute to your numbers, and an employee might be an asset to your team even if their average dollar sale is relatively low, but there are also lots of ways to improve the score. It's your job as a salon owner to help every member of your team understand the concept, and increase their average dollar sale.

One of the things I love the most about coaching is watching operators grow in their understanding of this concept. This is one of those areas of visible change. All of a sudden everyone in the salon starts to talk like a business owner.

When you ask how business is, you no longer hear phrases like "It's a bit quiet", "It's a bit busy" or "We are flat out!" You hear responses that reflect a clear business understanding and a positive attitude, such as "We didn't have as many clients as we'd have liked, however we recommended a lot of retail and the value of our treatment sales was up. Our average dollar sale was $138 and we made the most of our opportunities."

I love it! Now we can all seek just what is needed: more clients (and keep working on increasing that average dollar sale)!

So, how do you raise your average dollar sale?

The first thing you need to look at is the services you offer. If you just do eyebrow waxes, kids' hair cuts and other small ticket items, the average dollar sale will always be low.

Don't get me wrong! Small ticket items are important – and they are a fantastic opportunity to discover what other services the client might be interested in. Once you understand that 'From little things, big things grow', you will be grateful for all the opportunities that come your way. Building a relationship with your clients means that they trust your advice, and this leads into bigger opportunities.

We're in the beauty business, and we want our clients to look and feel awesome. There are always opportunities to up-sell – in the client's best interest. So let's start with the eyebrows. In over 30 years, I have never seen a set of eyebrows show up without a body behind them, so let's look at what else needs doing: let's talk to clients about what else they might want. Your client might show up for an eyebrow wax, but if you make other suggestions they could easily be interested – at the very least it will get them thinking.

Once upon a time, eyebrows didn't have the emphasis they do today. Today they even have their own store! Ten years ago, you wouldn't have found a Brow Bar if you searched all over the city! Taming eyebrows is an essential service in my opinion:

my eyebrows don't cope with the native look at all! I employ three people on my eyebrows – I have them threaded, I have them tinted and I have them tattooed. I put heaps of thought and money into getting them perfect... and I guess you could add Botox to the list too. So if you offer eyebrow waxing, what else could you add that would increase your average dollar sale?

One of the most frustrating things I see in salons is that we often build a relationship with clients around everything except why they come in to see you, and we totally ignore the opportunities they give us. This is not even just about increasing the average dollar sale – it's also about increasing our clients' happiness!

Don't kid yourself that a client comes to you for his or her beauty needs and the rest is either bonus or BS. They don't know everything you know, and they don't even know what they don't know. Your job is to build a relationship with every client around the services you provide and the knowledge you have. To me, it's a bit like icing on cake. The cake is your ability, your skill, and the way you look after each of your clients – which is the real reason they come to see you. The icing is all the extra chitchat: the weather, or how Kylie Minogue still looks awesome. I'm happy for you to talk to clients about other things, but sometimes the cake is not very big, and there are buckets of icing running off the cake and onto the floor. That is a recipe for disaster! So, keep an eye on your cake-icing ratio.

OR

9

130　The Naked Salon

It's easy to get distracted from the opportunity, so in my salons we had a code for when a team member was over-icing the cake, just to bring them back to reality. We would either say "Is that your banana in the fridge?" or we would gently squeeze their arm. We developed the arm squeeze code because often there wasn't a gap long enough in the conversation to slide the …… code phrase in – way too much icing!

> *There are always clues as to what the clients needs are – if you look for them.*

So, it's your job to solve your clients' hair and beauty problems – and as you do so you're also increasing your average dollar sale. We'll talk more about the kinds of conversations you can have and the questions you can ask in Chapter 17 *Creative solutions that make your clients spend more with a smile*, but for the moment let's just look at the impact of these conversations on the value of your sales.

Your client asks for an eyebrow wax ($15 value).

Why not suggest having both an eyebrow and eyelash tint? And the client might say "Yes." ($45 value)

If you don't ask, you will never know – and you lose the chance of turning a $15 sale into a $45 sale!

The best part is that if you link your suggestion to the value it provides, your client will understand why you made the suggestion in the first place, and will know you are interested in the best possible outcome for them – not just in making conversation and getting them out of there.

There are always clues as to what the clients' needs are – if you look for them. The eyebrow client might say "My lashes are just not thick like they used to be; they seem to be getting thinner." You could then ask "Have you ever thought of having a lash and brow tint? You should, because you don't need to feel like this. When your lashes are tinted they look thicker, because when we tint the finer hairs in the exact shade they'll have that fullness you're missing. I can do it today if you like: it won't take any longer and you will love it. It will really make your eyes stand out."

If you genuinely care about your clients and are willing to learn some new skills, then your average dollar sale can't help but increase! Offering big-ticket items means that your average dollar sale will grow almost effortlessly. Give every client your undivided attention ,and care enough to share the knowledge and expertise that will make them look awesome.

How this works in practice

Maybe you're wondering what this looks like in a real salon, so let me tell you about Craig, a salon manager who just wasn't getting his team's numbers to where they needed to be. He was a great chap: honest and a pleasure to work with, but although he was doing a large number of clients, his average dollar sale was quite low and he was discouraged. You see, Craig specialises in cutting, and other people on the team do all his colours.

The thing that struck me when we looked through his figures was the enormous number of requests he got: no-one gets that many requests unless they're really good at building rapport with their clients! So I started asking him questions like:

"How is it that you have so many requests and yet you recommend so little home hair care?"

He thought about the question for a while and he didn't really know how to answer it.

I said "So, do you talk to your clients and advise them how they can repeat the style you just gave them? Do you talk to your regular male clients and ask them if their shampoo is free of laurel sulphate because of the link with hair loss?"

You could see the penny drop right there and then.

Craig said "I know what I do and it's totally the wrong way around. When the client is new, and I have not built a strong rapport so they don't really care about my thoughts, I talk home hair care

Later, when they've been coming for months (or years) and they really trust my advice I chat about everything else, except for what they need! When I think about it, that's about as silly as it can get."

We agreed that when Craig got back to the salon he'd put this discovery to the test. "I believe you own a Superman cape that you have never worn to work. You have more power over your clients than you know. So look after them like you know you should." I said.

About three hours later I got a text from Craig "First client in, sold product, rebooked and even upgraded him to foils, ha ha ha."

My reply: "So you found your Superman cape, Woo Hoo!!"

The answer is staring you in the face, but it's so easy for you to overlook it. Craig is typical of a lot of people I meet. His loyal clients love him and trust him to look after them because he has worked hard at building his relationships with them. But he really only does half the job.

You can guess what happened to his average dollar sale, right? It went through the roof!

You just need to work your magic one client at a time and the same thing will happen to you.

For more information and resources head to salonsmarts.work

To sum up...
How do you get these numbers and how should you use them?

As you can see, increasing your average dollar sale isn't too hard when you put your mind to it.

Your software will give this information to you, but it is so important that you and your team should be able to do the maths without looking at the software.

All you need to know is each person's total sales and the number of clients they saw to get to that total.

Everyone on the team needs to know his or her average dollar sales off the top of their head (as well as the number of clients they see each week and how often each client returns).

Post these numbers on the wall and track them from month to month and year to year.

Ask your team some questions about the numbers:

- Which team member has the highest numbers?
- Why is that?
- What can each person do to improve their numbers?

Celebrate your wins as a team and explore the reason for your losses. This will set you on a path of discovery because questions are the key to a great education.

If you focus on your average dollar sale and work on making it higher than it is now, you can't go wrong.

ten

10

Knowing exactly how much money you need to break even

Every business needs to know their 'break even' figure, and salon owners are no exception! You need to keep this number firmly at the front of your mind, and you must consider it in your decisions.

Just to be clear, I don't want you to *merely* break even – that's simply the point where you start to be rewarded for your efforts. For example, if your break even is $6,500 per week, then you only get paid after you've made $6,500.

When I had my first salon, my husband (he was a maths teacher) said "You just need to make $X every week and you will be fine." So I made $X, and it *was* fine, as long there was just me and I had complete control over everything.

I should have learnt the lesson then! Sadly, I wasn't interested – I just wanted to look after my clients and leave that sort of calculation to my husband. Why bark when you have a dog?

Stupid mistake! If I had bothered to learn it back then, I would have known what was really going on in my business. You need to stop guessing at your expenses and really learn what's going on from the start. When your team gets bigger, your decisions are bigger too and your numbers are even more important.

You need to know which staff are making you money, what training you are paying for, superannuation, taxes... the list goes on (and on) because there are a lot of expenses in any business.

Your break even figures fit into one document that makes all your numbers crystal clear. Once you have that, you can get on with the bits you love about your business.

This is a living, breathing document that changes as staff leave and new ones arrive, as you invest in equipment and make purchases. There are always changes so you put them in, tweak the original document and keep peddling. As long as you have a good understanding of where the money goes, you'll know whether you have the money you need to pay everyone, including yourself! The break even figures give you that at a glance.

> *If your break even is $6,500 per week, then you only get paid after you've made $6,500.*

Break even figures vs. profit & loss statement

My accountant was always keen to show me the P&L statement. Bless you, Doug! I used to take one look at it and point out something that wasn't right (in my opinion, at any rate). I also found it very hard to concentrate because his eyebrows were so out of control. Who on this planet thinks overgrown eyebrows are sexy...?

I am yet to agree with what the P&L says because it's a history lesson, not a forward planning document. My stock orders were paid every 4 weeks and sometimes they were paid a few days early, so it would show up twice in one month and make it all out of whack. As a score board your P&L is essential – but as a working document it's useless! It's finished by the time you show it to me.

The break even figures, on the other hand, interest me very much indeed because they show exactly when I start to be rewarded.

How do you get your break even figures?

Getting your break even isn't that difficult – even I can do it (and I couldn't create a P&L to save my life!). I have an easy electronic tool that is helpful, but a sheet of paper will do nearly as well.

The first thing you need to do is look over all your paid bills. Often when I do this with salon owners they say "Yep, that's cool, I'll get the book keeper to do this for me."

Not this time! I want you to do it just once, because it will be the turning point for most of you. It will be the first time in your business life that you have seen all those payments listed.

And I can just about bet you'll have at least one 'Aha!' moment where you go... "Hmmm, I didn't know that."

What you need to do here is to find every bill you paid over the last year. You'll look up your bank statement, credit cards, B-Pay and everything else you pay with. You need to track every last cent – from money spent on pots of wax to GST to taxes. When I found out the lump sum I paid the ATO every year, I was sure I was paying for all the major roads being built around my city!

Now that you have put this all into one document it will be clear to you for the first time. It's a bit like getting on the scales when you get home from your holidays: you know it's going to be the moment of truth. But it's just that first glance that frightens you. Then you know where you are and what you need to do next. No cake this week.

Actually, it's really exciting. It means that for the first time ever you understand why you seem to be going forwards then backwards. Like Nanna's rocking chair, you are always moving but you never even leave the veranda.

This tells you how much you will need before you even open the doors on Monday. What you will need every single week! So the break even in simple terms is everything that you spend on your business from the Christmas party and the rent, to the water rates and product.

I never really wanted to know the numbers, and in the early days I was fortunate that my husband took care of all that stuff for me.

Life changed for me and I needed to take on this role myself, or at least understand it, so that I could outsource it and still know how much money I needed to make in order for everyone to be paid, including myself.

What difference do the facts make?

When I start working with a new salon, quite often the owner tells me they don't take a wage. I look at them and think "OK, so where do you get your money?"

What they are often saying is "I have the salon's money and mine all mixed up." I usually hear "Oh, I take some from the salon here and there, but I still don't get a wage." So then we go through all the things they spend your money on – things for the salon and things for them. It's soon pretty clear that they do take a wage. And it's usually a pretty good wage. Often their mobile phone, home Internet and lots of other things like their car is being paid through the business. If they were working for someone else, that just wouldn't happen.

I was working with a girl in Ballarat. When we first talked she was adamant that she didn't get a wage. So I asked her if there were clear lines between her business expenses and her personal expenses. She admitted that she did use the salon card to buy things for herself – but not many.

Not only was this girl beautiful, she was also beautifully dressed, and I don't think I ever saw her wear the same outfit twice.

I challenged her to go through all the expenses, power bills and product company bills and put that all in the calculator. The next stage was to go through her credit card statements and highlight everything personal that she'd bought on the salon credit card.

Later that night I got an email from her with the subject line "OMG!!!"

Once she had added up every time she used the salon card for groceries or to buy her clothes, she realised that in the last month she had spent $1,800 just on her wardrobe. She liked to look good, but she just didn't realise how much it cost. On the other hand, she also saw how much her salon was actually paying her. It was the first time she understood what the salon was really making and we worked out that her wage was really about $1,200 a week. Not bad for someone not getting a wage!

What do you do with your break even figure?

Once you're clear on what your break even figure is, you can break that down into days of the week.

Say your break even figure is $5,700 per week. You're closed on Monday, so you have 5 days to make your break even figure, plus your own wage and some extra for future equipment upgrades.

Your figures for each day might look like this:

Tuesday	$1,000
Wednesday	$1,000
Thursday	$1,800
Friday	$1,600
Saturday	$1,300

That all adds up to $6,700 because you don't want your break even figure ($5,700) to be your goal. Adding an extra $200 each day means that you covered all your costs including a base wage for yourself. The extra is for other things you will have to replace in time: salon equipment doesn't last forever, and a refit is always on the cards (although I did see a salon the other day with a row of eight overhead hair dryers that had been there since the 50s, which looked really cool and trendy).

If you were trying to sell your business you would take these extras out, but as long as you are clear on what personal items you are putting through the business, you won't get confused.

The exciting part about having all your expenses set out in the one document means that you can see exactly what you are paying for. When I set it out like this I realised I was paying for things that I didn't really need anymore. It's important to look at every single item and see if there is any way to reduce these costs. Even just a little here and a little there adds up quickly.

We often think that we are winning when we increase our takings in the business, yet what we save can be even more important. It doesn't help you to increase your income from $8,000 to

$10,000 per week if you are going to be in exactly the same place financially. If you want to get ahead, the thing you need to work on is your profit margin. You do that by increasing what comes in and reducing what goes out.

To sum up...

How to calculate break even figures and use them

Go through all your bills and work out how much you spend week by week. Identify everything you spend on yourself and take that into account.

Now you know how much you need to make each week, you can break that down into the numbers for each day, adding in some extra for future salon expenses and personal expenses.

Then it's time to look through all those bills, and see if there are ways of cutting costs (there usually are).

If you do this diligently, you will see your profit margins increasing as fast, or faster than your income is – so overall, you not only get to enjoy more income, you also have a more valuable business if you ever wanted to sell it.

This is one time you don't want to leave looking through your bills up to your book keeper.

For more information and resources head to salonsmarts.work

eleven

11

11

How much are your discounts really costing you?

"Just make it $50!" How often do you hear this? How often do *you* say it?

This is a big reason so many salons struggle. I can't believe how many times I see someone rounding off! Why? I have sat in on countless seminars and webinars about how to run a successful business and I have never heard anyone say "Here a tip, round things off – your clients will love it and you'll be more profitable!"

So where the hell does this 'white ant' thinking comes from? For those who don't know white ants are termites. Destructive insects that quietly eat away at your house until one day you lean on the wall and the whole house falls down! YEP, you heard me... it falls down! It's the same in your salon.

11

Discounting is a terrible thing to do in any business and your salon is no different. I think that sometimes we blur the lines between a friend and a loyal client, so we are confused about who should get the discount. Well, sit down because I am about to tell you something scary. NO-ONE, EVER, GETS A DISCOUNT! (and yes, I know I'm shouting).

I truly don't think anybody should get a discount. To make it really simple, think like this: It's either full price, or it's free!

> **It's either full price or it's free.**

This is a really clear way to decide whether or not you should do it for less than the original price. I am not sure why people feel the need to discount. I have never felt the need. I give my clients my all – 100% every time – so I want to be paid in full. If something is $47 then it's $47, so why make it $45? Do you really think those two dollars are going to make any difference to the person you gave the discount to? Really? However, if you discount two dollars from enough clients each week it all adds up – AGAINST YOU.

So what do you do when this is rife in your business? Well, first of all you must be convinced that this practice is going to cost you serious money over time. Then you need to get the team to

11

understand that no good comes from this sort of thing. Even if you can't hear the termites munching away at your profits, they are munching.

I started working with a salon a couple of years ago and saw that they had set all their services at reasonable prices. But then I noticed that the average dollar sale was really low. So immediately I became suspicious. It's a beautiful salon. Great price point. Excellent work as far as I can see – so why such a low average dollar sale? Yes, they could introduce some bigger services and increase their retail sales – most salons can do that better – but why the low average dollar sale? It wasn't until I looked deeper and deeper that I noticed discount after discount after discount...

Family, friends of family, the person who once lived next door, same last name as family (no relation), and doesn't even have a family. Really??!!!

Family... well, I don't think we should be making money from our family. However, I think that your family can be the models you need to train your team properly. We all need models to train the team, and it doesn't mean they won't look good at the end. So send your family in for facials and other services-in-training, like haircuts and colours with the junior team members. It's great practice and can give us the feedback we need. I don't want your mother paying for her service. However, I think there need to be some guidelines.

Some salons have a 50% off policy where staff can nominate two people to their buddy list, which they can review only once a year. It could be your mother and your best friend or your sister.

11

Then anyone else can volunteer as a model in a training exercise for team members wanting to learn or improve their skills.

So, how do you undo discounts? Bad News: it takes time!

What do you say to someone who has been receiving a discount, large or small, possibly for years?

Try this: "I love looking after you, Sarah. It's always a pleasure. However, I have some good news and some bad news. The good news is that I have been discounting your service. The bad news is that I have been looking at my finances and it has been brought to my attention that I can no longer continue this discount. I have to charge you, what I'm worth, which is $45. Now, if that doesn't work for you I understand perfectly, and Jason, my first year apprentice would be more than happy to look after you at the price I was charging. Is that OK with you?"

If you don't have a junior, then you just say this is what the service is going to be. Most clients get annoyed that you gave them a discount, as they never asked for one in the first place.

I know that it can be difficult to address this problem, but if you don't take any action then nothing will get fixed. It really makes life very confusing if you have to decide who gets a discount and who doesn't. It also makes it very difficult for team members to reach their targets and it diminishes the way you perceive your own value.

The other day a salon owner was telling me about a client who comes in and has a blow wave twice a week for $25 (full price is $55). She's been doing this since she was a student and even though she is now an adult, she still comes in for the student price.

So my question was "If it's worth $55, why would $25 be an option?"

Yes, she's been coming in forever, but honestly the prices of most things have gone up.

Now the other issue we run into is the client who says "I want to come every week, so can I have a special price?"

Here is my standard reply:

"We're absolutely delighted you love coming here, and we have developed a program for exactly this situation. When you purchase a service in bulk and pay upfront we give you one for FREE."

So, you charge them for 4 services and give them the 5th one free. Or charge for 10 and give them the 11th free. It's up to you to work out exactly how this works to make your clients feel the benefits *and* protect your profit margins. If you do it this way you never have to monitor if she sticks to her part of the deal. It means that everyone wins.

I remember a few years back being in a salon where there was a special price for a 'little old lady' set. You know, the girls who wear pearls, fingers full of gold rings set with diamonds – the ones who tell you about the cruise boats they have just been on? Those poor, sweet little ladies who make you feel guilty when you tell them the price. Well, this 'little old lady' set and comb-up price was set at $30 and we decided to put it up to

11

$33 – just a three dollar increase. Then one of the girls piped up and said "Actually, I don't charge my ladies $30, I only charge $23." And another one said "So do I."

When we looked through the computer we found out that of the 16 or 17 ladies who had that particular service for which they were supposed to be paying $30, none of them were paying that amount. They were all paying either $23, $24 or $25. So how could we increase it to $33? The answer is we couldn't – not unless we were willing to risk giving at least two ladies a stroke, and have another two 'bag' our salon at the local Bingo. Every time you discount, you risk that happening!

> To sum up...
> ## What do you do about discounts?
>
> First of all, you really need to know what is going on in your salon. Those sweet little ladies I described earlier know their rights. So you need to take the discounts away gradually and explain the reason why.
>
> The other thing you can do is give them two options. If clients have been getting services at steep discounts, train your junior to perform them just as well as yourself. Explain to clients that it's now one price for the junior and another price for the senior. Let them choose how they want to spend their money.

11

I remember when I first got my salon's computer software. I cried myself to sleep a couple of nights that first week! I had managed to reach the age of forty without ever sending so much as a single email, and I was a total newbie. My new computer fixed a problem I never anticipated it would resolve. There was no more discounting because nobody could discount! To apply a discount you had to put a reason why, and we didn't have any. That slammed the discounter's brakes on so hard you could smell the rubber burning and hear the wheels screeching at the cash register. It really only took a couple of days before all the girls got the knack of telling the good news/bad news story.

Your best clients won't care whether you're discounting or not – unless they're mad at you for doing it without telling them. The other ones… well, if they won't pay anything that even resembles full price, you're better off without them.

For more information and resources head to salonsmarts.work

twelve

12

12

You wouldn't just 'guess' your colour proportions, would you?

It always fascinates me when I walk into a hair or beauty salon how few things ever get measured. OK, so we measure our hair colour, we measure the proportions in our facial treatments and we time things – but we don't measure how we're going from a business perspective. Why don't we measure those things?

Perhaps it's because we were never taught to measure – or maybe it's the emphasis on service and creativity. I'm not sure, but I know three things:

1. The only way you know how you're doing is if you measure.
2. Measuring doesn't diminish the quality of your service (I have a theory that it actually increases it!)
3. There's never been less excuse not to measure than now.

12

Anyway, the only way we know if we are getting better or worse is if we measure. I can't tell you how often I talk to a salon owner who tells me "This year is going really well! We're way ahead of where we were last year." – only to find when we look at the numbers that he's actually behind! Sometimes I also come across salon owners who are feeling as though things are going terribly, but when we look at the numbers they realise they're doing really well.

It's like losing or gaining weight: some people don't even own scales but they use their clothing as a measurement tool (almost everybody I know has a skinny pair of jeans that they can only wear when they are at their ideal weight) but one way or another they are tracking how they are doing. My Dad used to call this your 'fighting weight' – it's a boxing term, and to me it represents the best version of your physical self.

So, just like you track your physical 'fighting weight', I want you to know what your business' 'fighting weight' is. Unless you have a clear understanding of exactly what that is, what it looks like, and how you're tracking toward it, you are unlikely to achieve it. Measurement will let you know where you are up to.

I was working with a beauty clinic owner who desperately wanted to grow her team. Her team included herself and two others: one a full time and one a part-time trainee. She thought that if she had more staff the clinic would be making more money. She was feeling a bit flat, as we all do from time to time, and I knew that the number of people on the team wasn't the problem, so I said "Let's go back to this same month last year, and see how you were doing then."

Looking at the numbers, she saw that with the exact same number on her team she was consistently reaching and exceeding $6,500 per week, whereas the previous year it was only $3,500 per week. I knew that getting more people on the team wasn't the answer. What she needed to focus on first was getting her existing team to be more productive – but she needed to see the numbers to realise that herself.

You must measure carefully and often because there's no other way to know what is really going on in your business and what you need to change. You can start by comparing what you did this same week or month last year and thinking about whether you're working with the same team the same way.

Someone will tell me they have 5 people working on their team, and my first thought is "I wonder how many are making you money?" You have to know those numbers if you want your salon to be successful.

So, what do you measure and how do you know if your numbers are good or not?

I developed a way that makes tracking the figures really easy. I applied it in my own salons and I use it in every salon I coach, because you need to be able to look at everyone's performance at a glance.

I call it the salon's 'Health Check': they're the numbers that give you a snapshot of exactly what is going on. It's like going to the doctor. You might look fine, but unless you take a closer look (blood tests, a urine sample, or blood pressure test, for example) you won't know for sure.

12

I didn't have a computer when I started up my first salon, so measuring was definitely a lot of work. But most salons these days run sophisticated and very useful software that makes it easy to track your KPIs (Key Performance Indicators). However, I am often surprised by salons who have this great tool and just use it as a glorified till.

These are the things you should focus your Health Check on:

1. Number of clients seen
2. Number of retail units sold
3. Number of new clients
4. Number of lost clients
5. Your average dollar sale
6. Requests for a specific team member
7. Number of rebookings
8. What 'Focus' service are you working on? (This 'Focus' service might be lash extensions, facials or basin treatments – whatever you want to do more of)
9. Total sales

If you fill this in weekly, and spend time with your staff teaching them what these numbers show – and why they are important – you can't help growing your business. But if you don't bother, chances are your business won't grow nearly as much.

Every member of your team has a mini-business within your business. We need to help each of them become their very best – to reach their fighting weight – and to do that we need to measure.

- Weekly Health Check -

12

Name: _____

	The start date?	Week 1	Week 2	Week 3	Week 4	Week 5	Week 6	AVERAGE This is the total divided by 6
The total sales								
Number of clients								
Number of retail units sold								
Number of new clients								
Number of lost clients								
Average dollar sale								
Requests for you only								
Number of rebookings								
Number of the service you are wanting to do more of eg; facials								

Freedom of *Time* + Incredible *Team* + Substantial *Money*

the.zing.project 🌐 TheZingProject 📷

12

The only way to know if somebody is doing really well with your product sales or your facial business or your eyelash extension business is to measure how they're doing. And you really do need to look at them as mini-businesses within your business. Another thing this shows very clearly is how many people each member of your team sees, and that shows you what they're doing with their opportunities. It's good to see that two people on your team did ten treatments last week, but maybe one person only saw 12 people and the other saw 25 people. That reveals a massive difference in their conversion rate and tells quite a different story.

I love this Health Check document because it's the only way to know for certain how each individual is doing. And it helps each team member to track their own progress.

I was looking over the data of a brand new team I was about to start working with. I like to meet them one-on-one and ask them two things:

1. What would make this the best place you have ever worked?
2. What can I help you with?

This starts a conversation and we go from there. I go over their figures in their health checks and I point out all the things they are doing well.

I met with one girl in a team of 12 who was seeing an average of 26 clients each week, and had performed a basin treatment service on almost every single one. This was an awesome statistic, and I told her so, asking "How are you achieving this amazing result?"

To my surprise she got very defensive and replied "There is no way that any client of mine is going to have a colour fade on my watch! They come to me because I am good at my work and I know what is best. I tell them they need it and they say 'Yes'. I don't even ask now, it's just what I do."

She's 100% right! She has such a strong rapport with her clients and the knowledge to back up what she does, that she can pretty much do what she wants to service her loyal clients. Isn't that what we all want?

My challenge was that others in the same team – with the same basin and chairs, and clients from the exact same demographic – didn't feel this way: they were very quick to tell me that people living in the area don't have the money, etc. Same opportunities, different results: they just hadn't yet worked out that they're both the problem and the solution. That's where I come in.

There are 2 reasons why salon owners don't measure:

1. You don't want to put pressure on anyone.
2. You just don't know what you don't know.

I believe you can measure things in a positive way. For example, if you have a team member who wants to learn to do microdermabrasion, then I would suggest that before she even has a lesson, ask her how many clients she thinks she can realistically look after per week. There's no point investing time and money in training if they'll only service one client a week. Perhaps she thinks that she would be able to do 10 microdermabrasions in any given week. If so, where does she think these clients will come from? Everyone on your team needs to take ownership of his or her little business within your business (the entire salon).

If it will add to your salon's profitability, then doing the training is an excellent idea. However, if you don't set expectations and measure outcomes you are just taking a gamble. She needs to understand why you are going to offer this extra service, what it will cost the client and how completing 10 each week would change her overall performance.

Helping your team to understand the business side is where your future is. Surround yourself with passionate people who want to learn from you. I learned so much from my boss, Sam, because he bothered to teach me and I stayed there for 16 years because I was always growing and learning. The biggest thing I learned is that money is the prize. (I'm not saying that money is the most important thing in life, but would you do this if there weren't a significant financial gain?). That set me up to value what I did.

I have always had a huge respect for money and Sam taught me, when I count notes, to always turn them around to face the same way: he said it was showing respect. It seems just a silly thing to do, but it's an important business lesson. Have you ever noticed that the people who don't respect money don't have much of it?

Sam taught me to always say "Yes" to everyone who wanted a hair cut, and we would fit them in somehow. He was a bugger of a man, he'd say "Yes, take a seat, Lisa won't be long" and then grin at me. This is why I am so fast at cutting hair, because the seat where the men sat and waited was right behind me. I couldn't bend over for fear of a man looking up my rear end. Sam knew exactly what he was doing - sitting them directly behind me made me cut even faster. These days someone would call the cops! They were good times and we had fun... heaps of it!

If we measure progress we can see changes and praise it. This is part of my 'water and sunshine' approach: when you see something that you like and you want it to grow, you reward it with praise and it flourishes.

The Victorian Royal Childrens Hospital Appeal is a fantastic example of what happens when we compare this year's results with last year's results. Every year they focus on beating the total raised the previous year and every single year, they achieve their goal.

Measuring product

Nothing frightens me more than to see an over-pour or an over- mix, so it's really important that we get the balance between not enough and being wasteful.

Let's use hair colour as an example (although the principle applies to every product you use on clients). I think there needs to be a standard fixed amount that you mix. It may be 30 g or 40g of colour mixed with either 1 to 1, 1 to 1.5 or 1 to 2 ratio of developer so in the end you have a combined volume. There needs to be a limit as to how much you can use, otherwise your profits are being unnecessarily applied to someone's head – or worse, left in a bowl and washed down the drain. The only way around this is to show your team how much this is really costing you, and do an exercise that shows how much you save if you use 5g less on every colour for a week.

12

More often than not, your staff don't pay to have their hair done in your salon. I don't have a problem with that, but I say that in return they should be thoughtful about the quantity of product they mix.

A waste jar is a great way to get this started, although you can still over-apply product to a client's head so it doesn't seem like waste even though it really is. If you set the number of grams allowed for a standard application and then let your clients know that there'll be an extra charge if they need additional product. I have heaps of hair and I've been told this all my life, so I know this is common. Most clients are fine with this practice; they just want to be told what is happening. So you have a conversation like "Hi Debra, today I am going to be bringing the colour through to the ends, so I want to mix another 10 grams of product because I don't want to skimp. This extra mix is an additional cost of $9 – is that OK with you?" and Debra says "Fine". So you go off and mix it up.

The other side of this strategy is that you write in the history notes exactly how many grams of each colour you use on every single person. For example, 25g of 7.0 and 5g of 7.3 and 45g of 6% – you write it down exactly, so that it's easy for someone else to do exactly the same thing if ever you are not there, and also so that next time you know exactly what you need because if you needed to mix more, the notes will show it. If you took this approach with every single client, in about 6 weeks you would be using the exact amount on every client and it would save you time and a heap of money.

How this works in practice

I ask teams to challenge themselves to reduce 5 grams from every colour they apply, every week. This makes a huge difference to your total yearly product spend and creates huge savings. Sometimes I am shocked to find that the salon has no system for controlling product usage. In some cases they are using more than double the recommended amount!

> *The only way we know if we are getting better or worse is if we measure.*

When this happens I call it the "You can't possibly fix what you don't know" trick. As soon as people realise this, both owners and team members go on a mission to make sure everyone is doing the same thing. Waste can be so out of control that salon owners don't understand why they can't keep up; and feel they are just chasing their tails financially.

If you apply 40 colours each week and you can cut back just 5 grams on every application, that is 200 grams every week. In a year, that's 10,400 grams saved, or 104 x 100g tubes (173 x 60g tubes) you didn't have to buy. That is a massive saving, and if you explain that to your team they will be glad to help you.

12

There are so many ways that you can avoid waste! You only ever need one squirt at the basin, not two, so why not make time to explain the waste to your team: what they could be saving, and how to go about it.

My Dad used to get home after work and go from room to room switching off lights, all the way around the house. We could hear him shouting "Another one and another one! You kids are killing me!" Not once did he ever show us a bill or explain why he did that. He could have put someone in charge of switching the lights off; get us to experience what it was like to oversee a project. There could have been a prize if we got the bill below a certain level. It would have got us thinking about what we were actually doing wrong and why. Instead he just walked from room to room shouting "Another one!" as he flicked switches off. It solved nothing. Don't be like this, because it's costing you money.

There has to be a balance between the time you take and the price you ask. For example, I can do a men's cut in 20 minutes, and I can recommend retail in that same time. So I can look after 3 men's cuts in an hour. Some of you can only manage to cut two men's hair in an hour so there is a huge difference in your ability to make money. If you are a high-end salon and you want to take 45 minutes, that's fine, but it needs to be factored into your pricing.

Some men are happy to sit in your salon for 45 minutes; others would prefer to be out in 20 minutes. We get bogged down with thinking that good service has to take longer, which is simply not true – but you might want to consider offering both an express cut and a full service haircut.

If I am good at what I do and I don't muck about doing it, I can get you the results you want in a short amount of time. Since time is the one resource we can't increase, I think doing it in less time is worth *more* money, don't you?

If you asked your clients whether they thought that if they received the exact same service in less time, it would be more or less valuable. What answer do you think you'd get?

> *There has to be a balance between the time you take and the price you ask.*

For example "We can do your foils exactly the way you like them, only instead of you sitting in my salon for three and a half hours you could be out in two and a half hours? Would that be a good thing?" I'd bet you a chocolate cake that 100% of them would say "Yes". Now if you asked "Would you be willing to pay more for that?" You might not get 100% agreement, but I bet you'd still get heaps of interest.

12

The biggest complaint I hear when I tell people what I do is the time it takes salons to deliver the result. People might love you and love what you do, but do it in less time and they will love you even more!

I always had more than one person working on a client, apart from the hair cut. Happy to have two people blow waving. Happy to have two hairdressers foiling. But you must do it symmetrically. For example, if I am helping out and I place two foils in the right hand side of my team member's client, when my client comes in I can't stop there. I need to place the exact same two foils on the other side. Then I can be excused.

I used to have two seniors doing a full head. You get your clients in, do an awesome job, and get them out. It's called teamwork. The resistance I get on this is huge, and yet you all seem to do it when you have a late client or someone is sick and you need to pull off a miracle, so why can't you make this a regular thing? If your clients could get the same result in half the time, most of them would jump at the chance.

It's your call, and I know some of you will be thinking "No way, we take our time." That's fine. I am writing this book because some of you are not being paid for the effort you put in and the time you waste is a big reason why many salons don't make any serious money.

For more information and resources head to salonsmarts.work

12

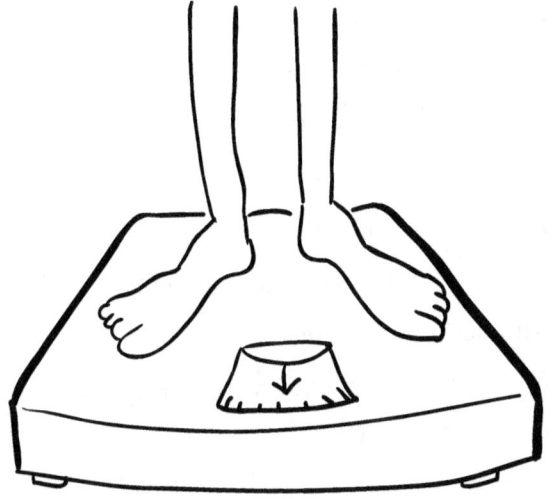

To sum up...

How do you eliminate time and product wastage and make more money?

Measure, Measure, and Measure! I can't say this often enough.

Reminder – check the following numbers weekly:

1. Number of clients seen
2. Number of retail units sold
3. Number of new clients
4. Number of lost clients
5. Your average dollar sale
6. Requests for a specific team member
7. Number of rebookings
8. Which 'Focus' services are you working on, and how are your numbers?
9. Total sales

Create 'standard' mix quantities and make careful notes of how much you mix and what colour it is for each client.

Have team challenges to eliminate waste (without reducing the quality of your service).

Consider offering a premium quality super-fast service (at a premium price). Advertise it and see what sort of interest you get. You might be surprised!

It's not rocket science, just common sense. The problem is, common sense isn't all that common.

thirteen

13

The 3 'R's - Rebooking, Recommending and Retail

This is the basis of any salon's success. If you get your 3 'R's right you would have to muck up big time just about everywhere else in order to fail. This is how you make money, and money gives you choices.

The 3 'R's of the hair and beauty industry are Rebooking, Recommending and Retail.

If you don't know how to hold on to the money, then that's a different story. Making it is one thing; holding on to it is another.

But if you ask me what is the first thing you need to do in order to make money in your hair and beauty salon, then I would say "If you are good at what you do (let's say that's a given), then learn to recommend."

People come to us for advice on how to look and feel beautiful and how to solve their hair and beauty needs. If you know your trade and stay up to date, then you can make intelligent suggestions with your heart and soul about what will work for them. You can't go wrong.

13

If you get back to the bare basics, it all boils down to recommending these three things:

- Recommend **services**
- Recommend **retail** and
- Recommend when they should **return.**

These three 'R's determine your future, your success and the consistency of your business.

So, how do you improve your numbers?

Every week at our one-on-one meetings I would ask each of my team members these questions:

1. How many clients do you look after?
2. How much do they spend with you on average?
3. When will they return?

The first time, they might say "I'm not sure." And I could live with that. By our second session they needed to have those numbers at their fingertips. It's really a core part of their training. One day, some of them will be running their own salon, and they'll need to know these things. In any case, as long as they worked in my salon I expected them to have those numbers ready for me, because if each member of the team could beat their own score in all three of these areas we'd be on a steady road to success.

So if you take the time to build your professional relationship with clients (talking about their hair, skin, etc.) and you recommend another service, they may come back sooner. If you recommend retail products they can use at home to fix their concern, they will love you because you are solving their problems.

Not only will they spend more on the day, they will also rebook because they will be grateful for your advice and recommendations. A client who leaves the salon with a booking is about 80% more likely to keep their appointment than a client who leaves without the next date is to call and make one.

How this works in practice

This is really just about recommending what you already know, the things that you take for granted, and the things that they don't know and will never know unless you share your years of experience.

There is a very old saying that says it beautifully: "They don't care how much you know until they know how much you care."

An American study reveals that if a client purchases one product from your salon there is a 30% chance that they will return; if a client purchases two products from your salon there is a 60% chance that they will return; and if a client purchases three products from you there is a 90% chance that the client will return. So there is a direct link between clients purchasing products and returning.

13

Clients don't purchase from people that they don't know, like or trust. That is why building rapport is so important. The trouble is we think that building rapport is about becoming their friend and the actual reason they came in becomes secondary to you (but not to them). You talk about everything else, their mother's Botox, their boyfriend's football game, where to buy a cocktail dress and killer heels to match. That's not why they come to see you, that's icing, remember!

> *They don't care how much you know until they know how much you care.*

I tell people all the time "Stop *selling*, and start *telling* people what your recommendations are." A lot of people are too busy today and they rely on you to share what you know, to make your recommendations. You need to be the 'go to' person. Learn the ins and outs of all things related to your trade so you can 'Wow' your clients with the results, and with the knowledge you share.

If you don't master the skill of recommendation you can still make a good living, but you will burn out. This to me is the most classic example of working HARD and not SMART.

I see this happen all the time: salons that don't make the most of the opportunities that are put in front of them. If you want to stand out, to be exceptional, an industry leader in the hair and beauty business, then you need to learn to recommend.

Here are a few creative examples:

Instead of asking "Do you want to rebook?" you might ask "When am I going to see you again?"

You might also offer to do something before the next appointment. For example, they might be going on a tropical holiday and you could suggest that they start the holiday with a spray tan.

It might be that they have a function on and you offer to put their hair up. Or apply their make up and do those smoky eyes that only make up artists ever get right. I don't know how many lessons I've had, but when I try to do it myself I still look like a raccoon!

I think if you knew that the client had plenty of time and plenty of money and was going to be interested then you would recommend more often. Sometimes you are thinking "I don't think she can afford it." So, if you don't ask her, neither of you will be embarrassed. I want you to consider this every time you are feeling uncomfortable. It's not your money! It's theirs. They can spend it wherever they want. It's none of your business – but it is your business to give them every opportunity to achieve the outcome they're looking for when they come into the salon.

I have a friend named Samantha. Our birthdays are just a day or two apart, and we have the same taste in many things.

However, there is one major difference between us – she would never buy a bottle of wine under $30. It's important to her to drink the best wine that she can afford. She would prefer a $50 bottle of wine but she doesn't go under $30 ever. Whereas I can't tell a good wine from a bad one and my limit is two glasses of any kind. If you took the fancy bottles away and did a wine tasting I don't have enough knowledge to sort the good from the great so I don't buy expensive wine – it doesn't make enough of a difference to me.

> *I don't think it's any of your business where people spend their money. It's simply your job to recommend.*

However, Samantha never pays to have a pedicure. She can't be bothered sitting there for an hour and having someone scratch about her toenails. She also doesn't think it's worth the money. While I love having a pedicure and I absolutely think it's worth the money.

When my children were babies I couldn't get to a salon to have a pedicure so I used to do it myself. I hate doing my own pedicure.I think it's one of life's luxuries to sit and while someone is doing a great job I can be fiddling about on Google.

The reason I'm telling you this is because Samantha and I are so alike in so many ways, but our money-spending habits are very personal. I don't think it's any of your business where people spend their money. It's simply your job to recommend.

Imagine if you went to a doctor and you had a problem and the doctor didn't recommend you to have a particular specialist or to buy a medication because he was afraid you might say that you can't afford it. How angry would you be if you found out from someone else that you could have had your problem fixed?

> To sum up...
> How do you get these numbers, and how should you use them?
>
> 1. How many clients you look after will depend mainly on your rebooking skill. It's also about marketing, but it depends mostly on how great you are and how much you impress them. If they have an awesome experience they would decide there and then to return. I keep hearing that they're all nurses, so they can't rebook because they don't know their shifts 6 weeks ahead. That's just another excuse. If you 'Wow' them, 9 out of 10 clients will rebook on the day. You can also suggest that they come back for a completely different service on a different day. It's just another recommendation.

2. How much they spend with you. You can recommend services and recommend retail products that will increase your clients spend and they will be happy that you cared enough to make the suggestion. The average dollar sale is the core success of your business.

3. When they return also comes under the category of what you recommend. You tell them when to come back, and once again, if you know your clients you will know when they are due in again. So in simple terms if you want to focus on your business these categories are the backbone of your success.

The trouble is that too often we think we are not in sales and that it's not our job to sell people stuff. That is totally wrong! It is your job to recommend whatever will help them achieve the outcome they're looking for.

For more information and resources head to salonsmarts.work

fourteen

14

Simple marketing that works for you

14

The best advice I can give you about your marketing is that you must keep it simple. If you make it complicated you will confuse your clients and your team – because they're the ones who are going to be answering inquiries.

When your offer is confusing, then the excitement and energy that you wanted to deliver disappears. Your team won't be enthusiastic about making the offer, so it will fail before it even reaches your clients because they either won't hear about it at all, or they won't be interested in it.

The second important piece of advice I'll give you is: If it works, keep doing it! Once you have an offer that gets results, keep using it – everywhere! Even if you and your team get tired of it, your clients and prospects won't.

Sometimes, you'll have a great offer that works really well for a letterbox drop, but not as a newspaper advertisement. Usually that's because the newspaper wasn't the right media for your message – you've got your message right, but you're using the wrong media. Most of the salons I work with find they get better results using targeted, local media delivery rather than broadcast media. Facebook works, some other online advertising not so well. You can test, but life is much easier if you just keep using the same offer – find out where it works, and keep doing it as long as it's bringing you results. (This is another one of the things you need to measure.)

For some reason we think that we need to change things all the time. By all means tweak it to get a better result, but changing anything just for the sake of change, is silly.

The simplest way to look at marketing is a way of **informing the public consumer about your product or services**: you are telling your business story everywhere – over and over. The world is full of messages and yours is just one. So keep repeating it and more people will hear it.

I call this 'The Dog Food Theory'. You met Muriel in the Preface. She's my second dog and she only ever eats dry dog food and mince. My first dog was a black Labrador named Stella, and she ate everything you gave her. I had Stella when the children were growing up and she ate whatever they didn't. Eventually Stella got old and died as dogs do. This time I wanted a dog that didn't shed hair so I got a Schnoodle (Poodle-Schnauzer cross).

I had no end of trouble getting her diet right. Table scraps either made her constipated or the reverse and I can tell you that you don't feel very much like 'the Master' when you have to scoop up something sloppy in the park and gag all the way to the rubbish bin!

If she stuck to dry dog food there was no issue. I had so much trouble getting my head around the idea that she could eat the same food every single day. I love variety! I am a woman *and* a hairdresser, so that's double the 'variety' boxes ticked there. I wanted to give my 'furry kid' some variety too. Muriel's vet said "You can learn this today the quick way, or not. It's up to you. Your dog can eat dog food only, or you can be embarrassed in the dog park. Your choice."

> *If it's working don't mess with it.*

The dog ate the dry food and never complained, so why did I want to change something just for the sake of change? The same thing is true with marketing. If it's working, don't mess with it!

So, how do you communicate your offer?

You want your team to be so excited that they want to tell everybody about the offer. So if the team doesn't understand the offer, you run the risk of it being a failure. This is not just costly – it's insane.

A great way to kick off your campaign is to do a 'Question and Answer' meeting with your whole team BEFORE you launch anything.

Give everyone a copy of the promotion, explain where it is going to be displayed and answer all questions with a 'Yes' or a 'No'.

- Is this offer for existing clients? Yes or No.
- Can this offer be used on a Saturday? Yes or No.
- Can the client use this offer more than once? Yes or No.
- Can this offer be used after the expiry date? Yes or No.

The clearer you are BEFORE you deliver it to the public, the greater your likelihood of success.

Whatever promotion you are running, you should always prepare a Question & Answer sheet. The meeting will flush out any questions so then you simply write them down on your Q&A sheet and ask everyone to sign off if they understand the details. I don't know too many people who read and sign documents without fully understanding them.

Another great test of clarity is to run it past an eight year old boy. If an eight year old boy can understand what the offer is, then it is ready for the general public – and it will probably be successful. I used to have two eight year old boys who were perfect for this. But now that Aaron and Jake are 23, I have to ask other peoples' boys to check the offer for me.

How this works in practice

I often get asked for ideas for effective offers. Here are a few ideas to consider.

If you are confident in what you do you could give away a service in order to win a long-term client. For example, if you know that you are really good at blow waving and you feel confident that if you gave away one blow wave service, your client might fall in love with your work and come again and again, that's an excellent idea.

One of my salons decided to put a sign up for that exact offer. The sign read "Free Blow Wave – Today Only!"

This caught the eye of a lady and she walked in to ask about the offer. It turned out that she owned a restaurant across the road. These two women had run businesses in the same street for over ten years but she only came in because of the offer in the window.

The hairdresser explained that she was filling a quiet spot in the hope of winning a long term client. She gave away a service worth $45 that day, but the lady was impressed and the salon gained a new client. This client not only comes in for a regular weekly blow wave, she now has all of the other services done there too.

These women can also easily promote each other's businesses. Everyone wins.

If you display this offer in more than one place you will get a wider response. The local gym, florist or even the dry cleaners might all be interested.

Keeping it only to the front window of your salon is thinking too small. If we want big things, we need to think bigger.

The gift of a free service is simple. It doesn't have 15 rules as to when and how, and that makes it more likely to work. If the offer said "Sarah is offering a free service on Monday till 2 pm. Advance bookings required. No GHDs... *and... and...*" lost me way back!

If you put your ad in the window and you don't get a response that day, don't just pull it down. Timing is important, so give it time to work. If it's not hurting you, you might just leave it there for years.

The really key thing with marketing is twofold: keep it simple, but think big. One offer. Many places.

For more information and resources head to salonsmarts.work

> **Keep it simple but think big.
> One offer.
> Many places.**

fifteen

15

How to 'Wow' your clients all the way to the till!

15

Never assume that your client knows exactly what they want when they walk in the door. And don't assume that they really want what they ask for first.

From start to finish you need to see yourself as a consultant, rather than a technician. You're not just taking what your clients say without asking questions and digging deeper. Even if you've been seeing a client for years, you should still be checking up to make sure their thinking hasn't changed, and if you've got a new client, this is where you'll either succeed or fail.

Many hairdressers are pretty good at doing this at the start of an appointment, or with a new client, but you really need to keep going all the way through to the moment they leave the salon. Almost every client I've ever seen or heard about are grateful for the attention and knowledge you share.

7 Key Components for a successful consultant:

1. Build rapport
2. Ask questions and listen to the answers
3. Make suggestions
4. Use visuals
5. Link the outcome and the value
6. Explain everything you do, and the reason for doing it
7. Close the sale

Have you ever finished a treatment and had a client say when you finished "That's not what I wanted!"? It's a horrible feeling! If you follow these suggestions you'll never hear anything like that again. Truly, if you give people what they want they'll keep coming back forever, but the only way to find out what that is, is to talk to them.

So, how do you 'Wow' your clients?

1. Build rapport

This is all about making your client feel comfortable with you so that they can really listen to your suggestions. If you don't build rapport with them quickly the chances are they will leave looking pretty much the same as when they arrived – even if that's not what they really want.

The most effective way to build rapport is to put yourself in your client's shoes and consider the world from their point of view – that's what I mean when I say "The Naked Salon". You need to listen, and listen carefully! Ask questions about their previous salon experience, their hair and skin care regime and listen for clues.

Did you hear what I just said? Most of us talk about movies, pets and restaurants with our clients, not about the things we're expert in – the services we provide, and our clients' needs in those areas – the reason they're in our salon in the first place!

> *Put yourself in you client's shoes and consider the world from their point of view.*

If a client said "Last time I went to the salon it was $80 more than I expected" you know that they probably want to know what the cost is upfront – or at least along the way. They may tell you that the last beauty therapist was so made up, or so punk looking, they felt that was what she was pushing them towards. If you hear that, you know you need to reassure them you're trying to make them look their best, not your idea of what looks best.

I've had clients who said "No" to everything I suggested. So, I turn it back to them. "You seem to know exactly what you want. You tell me what you'd like me to do." Often they end up asking my opinion as we go along.

2. Ask questions and listen to the answers

This is vital! By asking questions you're directing the conversation where it needs to go.

Questions that can be answered with a simple "Yes" or "No" are important, but so are questions that require your client to tell you more. You can draw out your clients with something like "Tell me a bit about how your hair is feeling today" which will give you more information you can use to make suggestions, or "Did you shampoo your hair this morning?" "How often do you shampoo your hair?" This will give you precise information that helps you understand more about how their hair behaves and what they want.

"Why?" questions are great for really learning what's going on in the client's mind because sometimes when they say what they want, they're making assumptions about what you can really do for them. It's your job to learn what you need to know so that you can give them a style they love and can manage. You're the expert, so you need to lead the conversation.

Role-play is the only way to teach this and it can be a lot of fun – so add that into your team meetings and watch everyone improve. Listening is a long lost skill and 'NOT-listening' is rife in hair and beauty salons. We were given one mouth and two ears for a reason – we all need to listen twice as much as we speak!

3. Make suggestions

People who make suggestions are the ones who usually end up doing the work they love. If you don't care about your clients, you just do what you're told – people only make suggestions when they actually care about their work and the outcome they create.

You don't have to suggest huge changes – you might suggest that you just tidy up the ends today, and after the wedding, or on their next visit they think about a completely new look. Then you might show them some pictures. Perhaps you offer them a sample treatment to take home and use after today's microdermabrasion to see what they think.

It's never a question of forcing something on them; it's simply not assuming that they know how to solve all their problems, and offering them fresh ideas. If you never suggest anything, then you won't have a chance to make a change they might love!

4. Use visuals

This one is so simple and yet it's often overlooked. I mean we're talking about how people *look*!

Before-and-after photos are awesome for helping clients see exactly what they can expect. It really doesn't make sense to write pages of instructions when a picture is much easier to understand, and much less subjective. Even for people who like instructions (and women typically prefer illustrations), this is one area when pictures work brilliantly!

Let's take skin needling as an example. For about 24 hours after treatment, a certain amount of redness and swelling is normal. Show your clients a photo or two and say "This is what you can expect to happen. It's normal." So then, the next morning when they look in the mirror and their face is a bit red and puffy, they can say "This is OK." or "Wow; I'd better call about this reaction!"

Or take colour (as another example). Simon, my gorgeous man calls me, amongst other things, "Little Red". He describes me as having *red* hair. My sister heard him say this when we were on the phone and asked if I had changed my hair colour. My hair is a Copper (8.44 for those who understand that term); he calls that red. My sister thinks red is a cherry colour (say 6.56).

So, colour is really easy to show, but much more confusing to describe. I like working smart, so I'll use a 3-second photo rather than a five minute conversation, at the end of which we might still not understand each other.

I think that we keep away from photos because we think our clients will expect an exact result. But we're not using them that way – we're using them as one tool in our toolbox. I had as many examples of bad hair in my collection as I did good ones, because it makes it quicker to pin point what clients want and what they don't want. Pictures are fantastic for explaining why the style a client is set on is not a good idea for their particular hair type, face shape, or neck length.

Sometimes clients just haven't thought things through, but you can use a visual to demonstrate. Have you ever noticed that ladies with *NO neck at all* choose the images of the ladies with long elegant necks? I saw that all the time – and it was my job, to use an image to gently explain that if you're a hippopotamus you can't wear a giraffe hairstyle and expect to look your best.

Create your own salon stylebook (with the help of your team) and have lots of images of blondes and fringes, men's styles and, elegant hairdos, celebrities, different face shapes and so on. You want to be able to show clients how someone with their face shape will look with a fringe or without one, and so on. You also want beauty photos – before and after, make-ups, eyebrow shapes, nail finishes... the list is endless!

These days you can do that on an iPad and it's probably more professional than the ones I used, but you still need to find the images, organise them and use them with your clients. Back when I was working in the salon, when someone came in for advice I would often do a consultation there and then. Then I would make notes on the computer so that when they came in for their appointment we could quickly pick up where we had left off.

You won't believe how much easier pictures make your consultations – and how much happier your clients will be with results!

5. Link the outcome and the value

So now you gather everything you've discussed previously and pop it into one sentence like this:

"So, today I will be doing your foils a lighter shade of blonde still in the creamy wheat range that you like, and I'm also going to give you a solid fringe to frame your face, how does that sound? I just can't wait to see how much younger you'll look, so lets get started."

This gives your client a chance to say if that wasn't how she saw it unfolding, or maybe to say "How much will it cost?" and ask any extra questions she has.

This way you are both clear and all is good with the world.

6. Explain everything you do and why you are doing it

It drives me silly when I hear about situations where there is a mountain load of confusion! All you need to do is talk about what you are doing and why. You can start with how long things take to process.

"I will leave you here and Aaron will get you a coffee. Foils can take anywhere between 35 and 50 minutes to process – it really depends on your hair, so Aaron will take a look at 35 minutes and keep an eye on them until they are absolutely perfect and ready to rinse." That way she's expecting Aaron to keep coming back to look, and doesn't get scared by it.

When you talk about what you're doing, it also lets the client know that you are tailoring things especially for her. For example, I usually put the hairline foils in last, after I have done all the other foils. Why? Because the hair around the hairline is really a lot finer than the rest and it takes much more quickly. You probably do the same thing, but do you share this with your clients? It really lets them understand your thoroughness and expertise.

This is especially helpful when you're at the basin shampooing their hair. You're explaining what kind of shampoo you're using, why you're doing it twice and so on. I'm so used to doing this that I even explain it when I shampoo my dog Muriel (who has two shampoos a week). The other day my daughter was downstairs listening in, and she said "You know that Muriel isn't going to buy any shampoo from you, Mum."

I said "It's funny, I wasn't thinking about it, sharing what I know just comes automatically." OK, now I am telling a dog what I'm doing – she is part Poodle, so she's really more like a furry child than a dog!

The thing is, I am not doing it for a sale; I am doing it because I believe it's a crime that we don't share what we know. We have a huge amount of knowledge that we just take for granted – and that's just madness!

Talk to clients and let them know how many times you are thinking specifically about them and their hair or skin type. You'll be amazed at how much of your knowledge you get to share, and how much happier your clients will be with the result.

7. Close the sale

This topic is one of the hardest things for a lot of you, because you don't want to appear pushy. I get that. However, clients want you to help them decide what to do because you're the one who knows. When you develop rapport with clients, they trust you. They are just happy to let you decide for them.

"If I could achieve the blonde that you want, is that something you'd like me to do for you?"

"Yes."

"Would you like me to do it today?" "Please."

Closing the sale is about asking permission, it's the obvious next step because you've already established what they really want.

Imagine if you are out at a bar and you are chatting to a girl and you seem to hit it off, she thinks your jokes are funny, that's always a good sign. You chat away and things are really great. Then her girlfriend comes over and says "I'm going now. If you want a lift home you'll need to come right away!"

This is the awkward part. You want to see her again – she might be thinking the same. So someone needs to say something or you'll never know. So you say "Did you want to see the film we were talking about? I am free this Tuesday if that suits you." YES! That is closing the sale. You might get a "Yes" or a "No", but either way you won't die wondering.

You just have to ask. The only way to make it easier is to try. Trust me, the more times you do it the better you get at it.

When I was a kid we had a pony called Lucy, and my Granddad taught all nine of us to ride her. He told each of us right from the start, that no matter how many times we practiced we would never be any good at riding until we had fallen off ten times. We all understood that falling off was a good thing! In fact, I can remember thinking, as I picked myself up and wiped the dirt off my face "Oh, cool! I am one fall closer to being a good rider."

So, start practicing. You'll fail some and you'll close some, but you'll improve every time you try.

As far as the pony went, I only fell off twice before I decided "Nah, not for me." I was thirteen by then and decided that boys were more fun than horses.

> To sum up...
> How do you 'Wow' your clients at every step?
>
> Never assume anything about your clients. It doesn't matter if they are perfectly groomed or if they look like a mess – talk to them about what they want, and how to look after their hair and skin.
>
> Keep making suggestions, because a lot of the time your clients don't know what they don't know. They may look great, but want a different look – or something easier to manage. If you talk to them you'll learn what they're looking for.
>
> Role-playing with your team is the best practice you can get – and then try it out on every client who walks into the salon.
>
> If you use my 7 Key Components from the moment they walk in and set the expectations, and then keep talking about what you're doing all the way through your service you can't go wrong.

For more information and resources head to salonsmarts.work

15

sixteen

16

Unhappy clients, bad clients and common mistakes

16

We all lose clients. Some move too far away, and there's a limit to how far people will drive for even the best hair or beauty treatment. Some clients die – just to avoid coming back to our salon! (I think that's a bit extreme, but what can you do?)

What I don't understand is when a salon owner doesn't know, on a week-to-week basis, exactly who hasn't returned and why. This is essential knowledge! You can even call them up and ask – especially if they've been coming for a while. You also need to track which members of your team are retaining clients and which aren't. This might be awkward, but it's essential information if you are going to increase the number of clients you retain. It's one of the biggest factors in your profitability – and a high retention rate will definitely help you to sleep at night.

I see a lot of salon owners who are trying to build their business, so they start to spend less time working on the floor and move some of their clients over to another team member. This happens all the time, and it's actually a good thing in many ways, but you need to measure if your client is happy with the change. Does the new operator retain the client? In one salon, the owner took time off when she had a baby and although the clients came in to see the replacement therapist once, most of them weren't coming back for seconds. The girl who took over her clients was not at all like the owner and blind Freddy could see that it just wasn't going to work. But the owner had no way of knowing what was happening until the clients had well and truly moved on.

Most clients leave in absolute silence. If you're really lucky, your client will ring and tell you about her experience. I love that, but some people find it hard to cope with. As far as I'm concerned, it shows me that they see you are serious about the service you provide, and it even gives you a chance to get them back. If they don't say anything, you don't have a second chance. So unless they are a D-grade client (more about that in a minute), use this as an opportunity to change the outcome.

So, how do you track your retention rate?

Your salon software will help you with this, but it's your job to use it to keep an eye on this number. You can't just wait for complaints, because most clients won't complain. They'll just leave quietly.

I work on 16 weeks between visits (others prefer 12): if you haven't seen a client in this period then you should activate your 'lost customer' program. I strongly recommend that you have a clear system in place to make contact with these clients. You can do lots of things here: send an SMS, send a letter by post, even make a phone call. It could be a simple reminder, or a special offer. The best solution depends on your client base, and the particular client who isn't returning (sending an SMS to Nanna is a bit silly). The main thing is you get in touch with them.

> *Keeping clients happy is ideal, but winning back a dissatisfied customer is a greater achievement.*

16

You don't even have to wait until they haven't shown up for a while; you can make it part of your service, especially if they are a regular. It shows you notice them, and don't take them for granted. Luxury car dealers like BMW do this every time, just to make sure you are happy. My dentist even called me once. It was a few hours after he'd done a root canal. I couldn't really talk to him, but I think it showed he cared – my wallet was empty, but it was a nice touch just the same.

Keeping your clients happy is the ideal state – but winning back a dissatisfied customer sometimes feels like an even greater achievement. And you have to start by understanding that when a client does complain, it's really a compliment: they only say something if they think you will be interested in their opinion.

So, one day I received a call from a client named Judy, who had been to my salon just once. Judy had had her hair done and she was so disappointed that she rang me on my mobile (because all new clients received a new client letter in the mail a few days after their visit, which included my personal mobile number in case they weren't happy). I didn't get many of these unhappy phone calls, but I wanted to hear if someone wasn't pleased.

The follow-up letter had said something like "Thank you for choosing us, we are grateful for the opportunity to serve you. If you weren't happy with the service you received in any way, then I'd really like to know why, so please call my mobile on XXX- XXX-XXX."

Judy was not happy, so she called me to tell me about it – and I was grateful. I let her tell me about her horrible experience in the salon, and how there were 'holes cut in her hair'. (Don't you love that expression? I don't think I could cut a hole in a person's hair if I tried, but funnily enough I have heard that more than once!) Anyway, I let her talk until she ran out of words, then I asked her who the hairdresser was – and got the shock of my life when she said it was Claire, my manager.

This didn't sound right to me, but Judy was furious, and she said the only reason she had bothered to call me was because my salon looked lovely, and my after-service letter suggested I was serious about the service I delivered. She was a business owner too, and felt I would be grateful for the feedback.

I offered to look at her hair and do whatever it took to make it right. Judy declined, as she was still too angry (I could almost see the steam still coming out her ears), so I just said "Look, the offer stands if you change your mind. Please call me when your next hair cut is due." And we left it at that.

I put the phone down feeling sick. I was cutting back on my floor hours and my thoughts were racing along the lines of "What the hell is going on when I am not watching?"

I sent Judy a $30 bunch of flowers that simply said "Sorry we let you down." and I didn't even get a "Thank you."

16

Then I sat down with Claire and asked her to tell me what happened. Claire was my salon leader; she was awesome and she took her job very seriously. The clients were very important to her, and she was so passionate about getting things right, she used to make you uncross your legs while she was cutting your hair. (I couldn't care less, so on some things we agreed to disagree.) Claire was devastated that there had been a complaint – she even cried, which was really not like Claire. Like me, Claire rarely showed that she was actually human.

Judy had hair so straight it sat upright on her head, a bit like a baby's first head of hair. She had a home colour in a lovely shade of khaki level 8 – just a very ordinary, plain-Jane hairdo. That was OK, except that Judy came in with a picture of Halle Berry. (If you don't know who Halle Berry is, you really need to Google it.

She is one of the most beautiful actresses alive, and she has one African-American parent and one white American parent.)

Judy must have asked one too many questions and Claire wasn't wearing her 'patient shoes', plus the home colouring would have sent her over to the snitchy side.

So there was nothing to do but wait and hope she'd give us another chance. One day out of the blue, Judy rang and said that if the offer was still available she would like to try my salon again.

"You beauty! Game on." I knew if I looked after her myself she would be a happy client, however I needed to believe in my team too. So I went for the 'big stretch' and decided not to do this haircut myself.

16

Judy came in and I met her and thought "Halle Berry, mmmmmm?" but I just introduced her to Stacey, my third year, who was ready to do what ever it took.

Stacey did a little trim, talked about adding some foils – I think she said "highlight the existing blonde" (It was khaki, but Stacey always made people feel good – love your work here Stacey!) and Judy left paying for the foils only.

Some months later, I popped into the salon and Judy was there in the waiting area. She was waiting to see Stacey, so I sat beside her and we chatted about the weather. Then she put her hand on my knee, looked me in the eye, and thanked me very much for listening to her. She said "I was right, you do care about your clients."

Damn right I do!

But there's another side to this...

We can waste a lot of effort and energy trying to please D-grade clients. Some people can never be pleased, and you would be better off if they went somewhere else. They make us feel undervalued and we rarely get any satisfaction from looking after them. Since most of us want to please everyone. we see these clients as a challenge – and for some strange reason we expect to be able to please everybody. You are much better off giving them their money back and getting them out of your salon once and for all. I only ever asked four women to not return in thirty years, but I was glad to see the end of each one of those.

This is the way I see clients. They come with letters in front of them: A, B, C or – if you are unlucky enough – D. Once you learn this, it really sets you on your way with a challenge to upgrade every client to the next level.

An A-grade client is pretty easy to spot. They love you and your work. They are always on time, they pay their account on the day, they never whinge, and they tell you that they couldn't live without you. They also insist on booking their next appointment and everything else in their diary works around you. They recommend you to their friends and they purchase products from you, too. They follow your instructions about looking after their hair and beauty needs between visits. They are the reason we do the work we do. Right?

A B-grade client does most one of these things, but not all of them. Maybe they never rebook on the day.

Your C-grade clients are missing 2-3 of these qualities: maybe they don't rebook, they never buy retail or they occasionally show up a few minutes late.

The D-grade ones… well, let's just say they are trouble, and to be honest, they are really not worth the effort. They're the ones we spend most of our time complaining about when really we just need to move them on. I've always said that 'D' stands for 'Don't Do', 'Drainer' or 'Donut' (more holes than substance).

My eldest sister explained the 'Donut Theory' to me years ago.

I was complaining about one of my sisters-in-law (I have five, so the chances of one being annoying are high). I wanted to gather the whole family together, and I was spending a lot of time on the project and feeling under-appreciated. My sister took me aside and said "Our family is like a donut."

I said "Huh? *You're* the donut! What on Earth are you on about?"

"You are focusing on the thing that they aren't – the bit that is missing." If someone gave you a donut, would you say "Hey where is the bit in the middle?" No, you would just see it for what it is, say "Thank you" – and pop the kettle on.

So the D-grade client is the one that we go on about. They can actually ruin a great day's work if we keep going over our time with them in our head. Just accept that we are going to come across people we can't please and move on.

You need to just see it for what it is. D-grade is not your focus. Just work hard on upgrading your B-grade and C-grade clients.

Can you really upgrade your clients?

Yes, you can! Let me share a story...

We had a regular client who often rang on the day he wanted an appointment and slotted in with anyone who had the time. His name was Maurice and he always stood at the front desk while he waited. The girls would greet him, he'd tell them he was here for a haircut and he would stand at the desk and wait. It drove the girls nutty that he would not take a seat.

Really? I couldn't care less. If you were concentrating on your client, you shouldn't have noticed.

Maurice never took a seat. He always stood and watched while he waited. He was in his early fifties, and to a bunch of girls barely twenty, he was an old codger. This day, Maurice landed in my chair.

We got chatting about his hair and he mentioned he had a family wedding coming up, so he wanted to look a bit smart. He was going out to buy a new suit straight after the hair cut. I suggested that if he liked, I could do this great little trick that just coloured the very tips of his hair. That way it would look sun-kissed, not coloured. Everyone would just think he has had a holiday in the sun.

Maurice liked the sound of that. "Why not?" was his reply, and I got on with creating the new look.

I think a haircut back then was $35. The colour on the tips was another $35. Now because he was a smidge blonde and was going away, I talked him into getting a shampoo and conditioner that had a slight purple tinge, to keep the blonde perfect. Maurice had never even used conditioner before and so after talking to him about what he needed he left with a colour, a haircut and some product. He did think he was a bit fancy. He thanked me more than once for the effort I had gone to. "Just doing my job" was my standard reply "but thanks for noticing."

Usually a $35 client, Maurice was now a $70 client and he now uses my shampoo and conditioner. As I was putting the payment through he thanked me for making him look like a rock star (his words not mine) and I said "So when I can see you again?" Maurice asked "What days do you work?" as he wanted me from now on.

16

> *How can you best serve this person and their hair or beauty needs?*

I said "Well, you will need to book now to get me." He explained that he doesn't book because he travels overseas regularly and he would find it hard to keep his appointment. So I said "Why don't you make the booking now, and I will SMS you two days ahead to see if the booking still works for you. If you don't need that appointment, we can always give it to someone else. How does that sound?"

"It's a deal" said Maurice.

It really is that easy. The girls were more concerned about his annoying habit of standing at the counter and not about how they could best look after his needs. This happens all the time and it drives me mad. We miss opportunities all day every day. We need to be asking ourselves "How can I best serve this person and their hair or beauty needs?"

For more information and resources head to salonsmarts.work

To sum up...
Upgrade your clients and track your retention rates

Think about what letter the client already is, then challenge yourself to raise the standard just one level. So your Bs become As, and your Cs become Bs.

If you have a clear picture of what an A-grade client looks like, then you can grade every client and set yourself the challenge of adding just one more characteristic each time they come in. It becomes a game you play with yourself.

Remember Maurice, and do this for every client in your chair. In most cases, if you bother to explain why it is you want to do this to their hair and paint the big picture, (sell the sizzle not the sausage) people will love the fact that you have thought about what would look best, and in minutes you have a plan. Everyone loves a plan. It's that easy.

The other really key characteristic of a successful salon is that they track their retention rates very, very carefully.

You won't believe what a difference to your profitability just upgrading your clients and finding out why people are leaving will make!

16

seventeen

17

Creative solutions that make your clients spend more with a smile

17

We all want to make more money, but none of us wants to be a 'pushy salesman'. Even if you are tempted, remember that while selling more makes your salon more profitable, your clients are your biggest asset – so you never want to be pushy. If you are, they won't come back – it's that simple!

The most effective way I've ever found for making my clients spend more money with a smile is the 'Suggest' thinking.

One of the biggest complaints I hear from clients about their beauty therapists and hairdressers is that they are disappointed they never get any suggestions. It's just the 'same old, same old', and this is certainly a slow death.

17

I believe there are three mindsets when it comes to the people who work in our industry:

1. "Same again?"
2. "Yes, I can."
3. "I suggest…"

And let me tell you that you need people with the third mindset in your salon if you want your clients to spend more and smile while they do it.

I'll explain a little more about these three mindsets. The 'Same again?' personality just does whatever was done before and plays it safe. Without even realising it, they are simply looking at how to repeat what is already there. They don't even try to find out if the client likes what they have and wants the same thing again. This shows a lack of knowledge and industry experience: a person who is too scared to do something different just in case it doesn't work out to plan.

I don't know about you, but I entered this industry so I could change the world, and just repeating the same old thing doesn't make any sense at all.

The second mindset belongs to a person who will do their best to create what the client asks for – but if they don't ask, they will be getting the same. I have seen team members talk clients *out* of things. I would hate to tell you how many times I have overheard someone ask about a shorter look, or a teeth whitening, and their idea is chopped down with an "Are you sure? It might go too …"

The 'Sales Prevention Department'? Honestly, I could cry. This is actually the most dangerous place to be, because if the client is set on a look they will try to create it by doing something they don't fully understand. This one can end in tears – the kind of tears that end up in legal action!

The third mindset is where we all want to be, and sometimes we go there. We need to spend more time here: suggesting changes, showing pictures, recommending treatments and products. Most of us do it sometimes, but not often enough. You're the experts. You're the ones in the industry who see new products and see possibilities in your clients that they won't see for themselves, so you're the people with the responsibility to make suggestions.

If you capture this way of thinking, and as I say "add water and sunshine" to it (to make it grow), you will take your business to a whole new level.

You can suggest that what you did last time looks great and you need to keep doing exactly that. Suggesting is simply taking an active interest – it doesn't mean you change things every time. It means you listen carefully and share your thoughts freely.

Tell, don't sell!

Nothing makes people switch off faster than hard selling. Beauty therapists and hairdressers won't sell anything unless they love it themselves, so you simply need to teach your team to tell and tell, rather than sell. If we share what we know and tell about the products we love, and the ones we think will suit each particular client, it will lead to a great relationship and probably a sale anyway.

Imagine you have a special promotion on. Say, for a month you are offering a free scalp massage with every colour. When you tell each client about that, you're simply telling, *not* selling. So you tell them that it's usually $18 but this month it's included with their colour. They enjoy the scalp massage, and next time they come in for a colour they ask for a scalp massage as well – knowing they'll be paying for it. Often in the salon we're so busy talking about the movie we saw last week, or who is cooking the Christmas dinner this year, that we miss opportunities to *tell* our clients the things they want to know.

New products, new techniques – even that we have a new whizz-bang coffee machine or the latest magazines. As professionals, it's our job to share our knowledge; to tell them the 'secrets' that will help them look their best. In that softly-softly process of telling, the selling will happen anyway, but you and your team will feel more comfortable, and so will your clients.

17

If you tap into your creative side and think about what is possible, get excited and make suggestions – then, and only then – does the fun begin! Whenever people talk to me about their experiences (as a client) in hair and beauty salons, I listen carefully. I especially love the people who say "My hairdresser wants to do A, B and C" or "My beauty therapist suggested I try X". I know those therapists or hairdressers are passionate and just doing their job, and this makes me happy.

So, how can you help your clients spend more – and love doing it?

Too often salon owners think the answer lies with some heavy marketing for new clients or a new piece of equipment. They know that something has to happen, and they are looking for a solution that will turn their business around. We do need to consider how we can spread our message more widely, and we do need to look at the services we deliver. But I also see too many times that we miss opportunities right in front of us because we don't 'suggest' enough to the clients who are already sitting in our chairs.

Nothing is more disappointing than purchasing equipment and not having your clients know it's there. That's where the power of 'suggestion' lies – and it's also the place for some deliberate promotion. If you suggested to every single client who came into your salon that they try out your new piece of equipment, some would say "Yes."

It is just a numbers game and the more people you ask, the more Yes'es you'll get.

I remember taking a chalk pen and writing on all the salon's mirrors:

M = :) ?

This doesn't really make sense until someone explains it to you: M is Microdermabrasion = A Happy Face :)

17

My goal was to get clients to ask what the chalk message meant, so that the team member had an opportunity to mention the new service. It was the perfect opening for her to go on to explain all the wonderful benefits to her client. It worked like a charm – the salon booked three treatments that same day. The chalk window pen was less than ten dollars.

You need to create a system for your suggestions because you all need time to practice those suggestion skills. I always suggest having a product of the month (or quarter). You then display that product somewhere conspicuously so that everybody who comes in the door gets an opportunity to be educated on that particular product. It's placed close enough to every chair so that it is a natural topic of conversation. Maybe it's a sunscreen and you explain the importance of using different strengths for your body and face. Suggesting a loofah for someone you are waxing is a no-brainer, but you could go further and offer a skin analysis free of charge next time the client comes in. It only takes a couple of minutes and it opens the door to looking after her skin.

How this works in practice

There was a lady who came to our salon, and she had a very ordinary little 'Nanna' blow wave just like everybody else over 75. She was quite a stylish lady and she had been having a regular blow wave, week-in-week-out for about 200 years (OK, maybe not that long, but for a long, long time!)

It was my dearest and oldest mate Neil, the local butcher, who had 'suggested' to Daphne that she come and see me. Neil was about 60, and he looked a bit like a silver fox. He used to walk his favourite customers out to the car, place their meat in the boot, and then gently say "Your hair does look lovely, but my young friend Lisa has just opened her first hair salon just around the corner. She is looking for new clients and said not to send any ugly ones, so I thought I'd send you. You will love her. I suggest you try her out."

That was it, and I think Neil sent me at least 15 clients with that same speech. Anyway Daphne came to see me. The first time I blow waved her hair just like she asked me to, but the next time we had a little chat about her style, since she'd mentioned the blow wave being a chore every week. Because she was a heavy smoker, she hated that she couldn't smoke in my salon. So I suggested we change her style and we talked about cutting it quite short like the actress Judi Dench. Daphne sat on that idea for a couple of weeks, then decided she was ready.

It looked awesome! Her hair was white as snow and she really looked like a brand new girl. It took a good ten years off her age.

> *You always get the clients you deserve.*

She turned to me and said "You've done yourself out of a weekly blow wave." Well, that was true enough, but I was never going to run a 'Nanna Salon', and the number of people who came in because of Daphne's new look far outweighed that repetitive weekly blow wave.

> To sum up...
> **Creative solutions that make your clients smile**
>
> If you want to change the clients and the type of work you do, then pull on your 'suggest shoes' and it will change – one by one.
>
> You always get the clients you deserve – so if you don't like the ones you've got, guess who you've got to blame?
>
> Have a look at how often you hear a suggestion in your salon. Make it your main focus and encourage your team to listen and then suggest.

For more information and resources head to salonsmarts.work

eighteen

18

Clients belong to the salon, not the staff

Let's get something straight about your team. They are all leaving; it's just a matter of when.

So, if you want to be an ostrich about it, then just bury your head in the sand and pretend it won't happen – and be surprised and disappointed every time it does.

We are in a 'feel-good' people-centred industry. We encourage our team members to build rapport with our clients because it's about the long-term ongoing relationship. The client not only loves you, they love what you do. It's a total package, so my best advice is to paint a picture of 'what goes around comes around' right from the start, and keep talking about it. Gen. Ys do get the Karma thinking.

It saddens me when I hear stories of staff members who leave and take all their clients with them. Sometimes they even steal the clients' information from the computer – and they don't just stick to the ones they serviced. If this ever happens to you, I can tell you first hand you will feel gutted! It can make you feel nauseous for days.

Can you ever protect yourself from this?

To be honest, no you can't. But there are some things that I have learnt that will give you a better-than-average chance of preventing it from happening to you.

It can happen to you. It happened to me, and I read in Tabitha Coffey's book that it happened to her too. She had four of her team leave on the same day, including her head stylist who had been with her for fourteen years, and who Tabitha had taught everything she knew.

When I hear a team member say "She is my client" it's like fingernails running down a blackboard. I cringe. I want you to realise that they are salon clients, and drill that into every member of your team. She is the salon's client; however she prefers to be looked after by Nikki. What that does is remind them day in day out, time and time again, that the client belongs to the salon, not to the team member – and not even to the salon owner. If you ever sell your salon, you hand over the clients with the business.

Change the way you address your clients so they get it too. "I am looking after Tess today" instead of "Tess is my client today." Tess is a *salon* client.

The only way that a client belongs to one team member is if a new staff member came to your salon with clients. When that happens, I suggest you make a list of these clients. That way you are making it very clear that when she leaves (and remember, everyone is leaving, it is just a matter of when) you have a list of the clients she's brought with her, and those are the only ones she takes.

Who the clients belong to is a question of mindset. If you are good at what you do, you can build a clientele, and you can keep growing your salon's clientele because most of them are leaving too – sooner or later. I always hired new team members without clients because I never wanted other salons to say I poached their clients. I made it an everyday conversation within our team: "The clients belong to the salon, you guys just look after them."

So, how do you make sure you're never in this situation?

There are a couple of actions you need to take so that you are never in this position. Share the clients across your team members – one person can do the spray tan and someone else the facial. Wherever possible, don't allow the work to be carried out by just one person. In a hairdressing salon, someone does the cut and another does the colour. I think this is an absolute must!

Even go as far as to have more than one person doing a blow wave: two seniors working together, for example. Don't just think about juniors working together, get the seniors doing it as well. This means it becomes normal for everyone to be sharing the work load and it helps you get clients out the door faster.

No matter how much they love you, they have busy lives and don't want to spend any longer than they have to in your salon.

Some people don't like this idea, and tell me "Clients come to my salon because we don't do this sort of thing". I want to be really clear on this point – you are putting yourself at risk with this attitude, so don't complain when a team member leaves and takes 'her' clients with her.

Six easy ways to ensure that you win:

- If your salon can do the service to the client's liking, and it doesn't take all day... **You win!**
- If your clients love you – and also love someone else on the team just as much – it doubles their chances of getting in when they need to, like at short notice... **You win!**
- If everyone in the salon not only says "Hello", they know the client's name and refer to them by name... **You win!**
- If the clients know your staff by name, and they feel like this salon is where they belong... **You win!**
- If your team members wear name tags and your clients know all of you by name... **You win!**

I remember doing an interview and a trial with a new team member. She was just what I was looking for: well-presented with plenty of get-up-and-go, and a great personality. She had been working in the city and wanted to work closer to home so she didn't have to travel. She didn't have her own clientele, and that was fine with me because my salon had clients ready for her to start working on straight away.

I offered her the position and asked her to read through my employment agreement. We could meet again in two days, sign the agreement, and start the following week. She called that night and I was disappointed to hear that she had changed her mind. She no longer wanted to work with me, as she didn't want to sign the bit about the clients.

My agreement stated very clearly that the clients belong to the salon. If you come without clients, you leave without clients. When you finish you can't work in this same town for 12 months. You can work in the next town 15 minutes away, just not in my town.

I was very disappointed as I thought she showed great potential. She got a job in the next town and worked there for two years. Then she left suddenly, taking all the clients she had been working on for the last two years to her new salon, which she opened up just across the street. I don't know about you, but I think that was her intention all along. She'd have done the same thing to me except that I made it very clear the clients belonged to the salon.

All I did was make it more difficult for her, or at least highlight the obvious fact that I meant business.

The problem is we are always looking for the good in people, and that is the reason we chose this career. I don't want that to ever change. However, you do need to say what you mean, mean what you say and don't ever be mean when you say it.

If my directness and clarity means I avoid situations where people don't understand what I want from them, then it's a good thing.

Most people don't want to hear the truth or the facts unless they're pleasant. I get that. That plays a big part in explaining why there are so many salon owners working hard and not making much money. It's the politeness – the 'NICE' – that kills us.

NICE stands for:

Nothing
Inside me
Cares
Enough

...to tell you the truth.

But I *do* care about you and your salon, and I want you to be really clear with your team that the clients belong to the salon, not to any single individual.

My hope is that after reading this book you will know there is more to learn, more to consider, and agree that perhaps you don't know everything. I've always believed that "When you're ready to learn, the teacher will appear".

> *When you're ready to learn the teacher will appear.*

That is why I felt the need to share, because when you take your 'I know about that' heels off and wear your 'show me how that works' boots, a whole new world will appear. You can keep whinging about what a huge industry problem this is and how you can't ever protect your hair and beauty salon from losing clients when a staff member leaves – or you can take the other option and do whatever you can.

> To sum up...
> How do you get this message across?
>
> You need to be upfront about this with your staff if you want to minimise the risk of them taking clients when they leave.
>
> My staff agreement was one very definite thing that helped. Once they signed that, we all knew where we stood.
>
> Your life will be much simpler if you hire new team members without any clients: that way they come without clients and they leave without them.
>
> Make it an everyday conversation – the clients belong to the salon, team members just look after them – and make sure that more than one team member is looking after your clients.

For more information and resources head to salonsmarts.work

nineteen

19

A-grade clients make your life a joy – but you may not recognise them at first glance

The answer to your hair or beauty salon's success is simple – in fact, it's so simple we overlook it all the time. It's all about the care and attention you give each of your clients every time they walk in!

Creating an A-grade client is really just a question of making sure there is no gap between the customer service your client expects and the actual customer service they receive. To put it bluntly, most of the time all you and your team need to do is 'shut up and get on with servicing the clients'. By servicing your client I mean thinking about what their needs are. What do they need while they're in the salon, what do they need to do at home between visits and what else might be useful for the client to know about the services you provide? It doesn't matter whether you are giving a facial, a hair treatment or any other beauty treatment. If you listen to the client you'll uncover their problem and solve it.

I've said this before, but it's so important I'm saying it again: "Everyone I know has been given two ears and one mouth for a reason. We need to listen way more than we do, and we need to talk way less."

> *It's all about the care and attention you give each of your clients every time they walk in!*

19

The trouble is, the standard garden-variety of hairdresser or beauty therapist seems to think it's their God-given right to yak-ity yak yak all day long. Good quality listening is rare. If you are so busy talking about the latest film you saw, the holiday you're planning or anything else that's on your mind, you will definitely miss opportunities to see where you can better service your clients.

The opportunities will still be there, but you will miss them. That makes your salon just like everyone else's. A friend of mine is a 'World Champion Chatter'. She is the only person that I can honestly say never has an off-day. She is happy 100% of the time. It fascinates me that she is always so happy – always! If chatting were an Olympic sport, she would be there on the podium, accepting a medal for first place. The medal is for continued talking without a pinch of listening. Then we all rise for the national anthem and yes, you guessed it, she talks through that too! Her husband says she talks and waits, then talks again, but he doesn't think she ever listens. Maybe that's her secret recipe for happiness – she doesn't take on other peoples' STUFF! Then again, she doesn't work in a salon either.

Have you ever had a listening lesson? I don't think listening is taught at all. As far as I'm aware, I certainly haven't ever had a lesson in it, but perhaps I wasn't listening while the classes were being held.

If you are to be a success in your business and make the money you deserve, you need to listen to your clients. Your focus needs to be on their hair and beauty needs, which is the reason they came to you in the first place, and the reason they will return again and again – and that needs to be true every time they come to your salon. I think that most people in the hair and beauty industry understand how important building a rapport is. However, sometimes we spend more time building rapport around the movies or pets we both own rather than the reason they came into your salon.

I remember one girl I was working with, who was building a house. That would be over fifteen years ago now, but if I went to her house I'd bet I could break in, because I know exactly where every room is and what colour it's painted! I heard her tell every single client about her house, right down to the size of the skirting boards, the colour of the paint and the tiles on the roof. No one ever called her on it, and she just went on and on.

Why aren't we policing this? Your clients don't need to know this stuff about you, although most people are polite enough to listen (and in any case they are trapped there for the duration of their service). They can choose not to return, though.

In my experience, the worst person in the team for this kind of yak-ity yak yak is the salon owner – which means that everyone else on the team does it too. What's more, I don't believe salon owners realise how much this is costing them financially – because if they did know, they certainly would 'shut up'.

This is a 'service industry': it's about servicing a client's beauty needs, and you can't provide service if you don't know what your clients want or need. I learnt from my first boss, Sam, that "Short of prostitution, you do whatever they like and charge accordingly!"

If they want five sugars in their tea, it's "Yes." If they want it all cut off, it's also "Yes."

You want a clipper cut that makes you look even more like a criminal? "Yes, come this way!"

Give them what they want!

I am not saying that you don't have a conversation when they are asking for something that might be a bit left-of-field, but what I am talking about is the idea that everyone should walk out with your version of 'fashion'. Your clients are paying you to deliver their choice of 'fashion', not yours!

So, how do you create an A-grade client?

One of my clients was a plumber named Dave who walked in and wanted a 'clipper hair cut', which I did for him. After a few visits, I moved him over to growing his hair a little so I could give him a much more stylish haircut. One day his wife, Andrea, popped her head in and introduced herself. She thanked me for sliding him over to the stylish cut he now has. By then I even had him using product and she loved his hair. A few months later, Andrea's hairdresser went on maternity leave and I got her as a client too.

Dave didn't start out as an A-grade client, but he became one because I listened to him, he started to trust me, then he took my advice. His wife was an A-grade client right from the start: partly because of Dave, but also because she walked in with a high level of trust in what we could do.

If you do great work, think about what your client doesn't know, and educate them to be the best possible version of themselves, you will turn almost all your clients into A-grade clients and it will change your business. But you need to listen carefully and make sure your relationship is first of all professional, and then social.

The conversation should be 70% client and 30% yours. That means you need to be listening 70% of the time. If the client wants, they can have their 70% in absolute silence. In your 30% you need to discuss what the plan is for today, what products they need to take home so that they look great until their next visit, and when their next appointment should be.

After you have addressed all of your client's needs, then you can have a light-hearted chat about your world. The clients still get a snapshot of what you are up to in your life, but more importantly they got their needs met first. If you implement this you will stand out from every other salon that doesn't, and A-grade clients will come running.

I've seen it happen over and over again and it's really all in how you handle complaints as well as how you service your clients. I knew of a chap who was a duty manager at the airport. In many ways his line of work was similar to mine. His job was to look after all of the service desks, all those points where passengers come in contact with staff. Check-in problems, expired passports, lost bags, that sort of thing. He was called out to speak to all the disgruntled clients. Ninety percent of the time the customer wasn't happy with the explanation they received: the person at the desk didn't explain the rules properly, or had an attitude about it, and the customer would get mad. So my friend would have to step in to 'put out the fire'. If the staff had been more considerate and showed some empathy for the passenger's position, it wouldn't have happened. It's the same in the salon. Most of the time, your clients aren't so much upset about the result as they are disappointed by the way they have been handled.

A-grade clients create an A-grade salon, and an A-grade salon creates A-grade clients. We had this conversation whenever we hired a new team member. I remember one new girl I interviewed. I decided to get her in for a trial and test out her skills. She seemed lovely, so I asked Claire, my manager, to oversee the trial. At the end of the day, I came down to chat with Claire and asked how the trial had gone. Claire said "She's fine, she should work out really well once she's learned how to listen and provide quality service." Claire and I both agreed that most staff didn't have the attention to detail we wanted to see when they arrived, but it didn't matter. We could teach that because there was such a strong salon culture.

New team members need to adjust to their new environment. The exciting thing is that if you create a culture of service, most of them will learn quickly and change the way they see and do things. When you are passionate about what you do, you will take on new ideas and find better ways to do things you already do well.

For more information and resources head to salonsmarts.work

twenty

20

Why did you buy a salon in the first place?

The hair and beauty industry is for individuals who love people and fashion, and who seek out how to look and feel the best possible version of themselves. It's also for those who want to do the same for their clients.

Most of us are always watching what other people are wearing and making comments on their appearance. We love the ability to change the way we look and we also understand that our appearance reflects who we are and how we feel. But it has become really clear to me that too many hair and beauty professionals burn out on this. They stop looking around for inspiration; they stop taking pride in transforming their clients – yet they stay in their jobs even though they are no longer happy in them. If this is you, and you are over the hair and beauty industry, then be brave and make an exit plan.

You really need to be honest and give yourself permission to move on. There are lots of things that you can do next: your training and experience is a good foundation for many other roles.

If you're not being honest with yourself, and if you're still unclear if this is your best career choice, take the time to look around at the 'over it' hair and beauty professionals – and ask yourself if you want to join that pile. If you aren't still excited about your profession at some level, then you will never excel and you won't regain the job satisfaction you once had.

I see it all the time in hair and beauty salons and other small businesses, and the signs are really easy to spot. People who are just 'over' serving other people. You hear them complaining about a particular incident or a particular customer. Maybe they saw 100 clients that week, but they go out of their way to tell you about the one horrible one. They are totally focused on the negative, and I don't know anyone who has grown their business by focusing on the negative clients.

They are easy to spot. In fact, some of them write signs on their door, so it is even easier to find them. There's a shoe repairer near me and I walk past his store all the time. He has a sign on the door, hand written in thick black pen:

> No Food or Drink in the shop.
> We close at 5pm Sharp.
> Pay when you drop repairs off. Cash Only.
> Please use the other door.

Well, at least he said 'Please'.

What the sign probably should have said was:

Why would you stay in a job you don't enjoy?

Two reasons:

1. It wasn't always like this. You slipped down the slope without noticing.
2. You just don't know where to start on making the changes you'll need to make to get out.

So, what are you really struggling with?

I see this desperation quite often in salons that are struggling. Owners will tell me how good business used to be, and how times have changed. They live in the past and they genuinely believe that people will no longer spend money on hair and beauty treatments.

That might be true... for them. Whether you believe you can, or believe you can't, you are absolutely right! It's your view of the world, so you own it.

The truth is we don't need 5 million clients. Most successful salons have an active database of between 500 to 1,000 clients. That's all it takes. If your clients are not spending with you it's because your passion and love for what you do isn't there and they're not feeling that energy which comes from the core of a person who loves their job. If you love your job, every day is great.

The trouble is, the world is changing at a rapid rate, and in any job you need to keep up with these changes. However, it's even truer if you are in the hair and beauty industry.

The services we offer are changing at an extreme pace! If a beauty therapist had suggested 30 years ago that she put hot wax on my 'pink bits' and remove every trace of hair, I would have called the cops. Laugh if you like! It's true: 30 years ago that was unheard of. In fact, I saw a nude painting in an art gallery just recently of a young lady and boy-o-boy she was extremely bushy down there. It looked very out of place. I thought "Lucky she didn't smoke, because that bush looked a lot like a fire hazard to me."

It's just another bit of proof that things are changing at a rapid pace and we need to keep up. You can stay doing what you hate and get grumpier and grumpier about it, but you'll have to work on your own because nobody could possibly work alongside you. I hear this one a lot, too: "I used to have staff and they just did my head in. It's better without them." Really? Isn't that interesting!

Most people I know get into a beauty business without any thought of why, when, or how they might get out. I believe you need to have a time frame and review your plan regularly: I think you'd be happier if you didn't just assume you'd stay in your salon forever.

You need to review whether you are being rewarded both financially and emotionally.

You need to think about what it is that you need to be doing in order to stay, and what is your line in the sand for moving on.

There are always going to be crossroads in our lives and we need to decide which road to take. One thing I know for sure is you need to not only love your clients, you need to love what you do to them. It's your responsibility to give them the latest and the greatest and if you can't do that it is time for you to move on.

I get asked all the time "Who does your hair?" It's quite sad that lots of people are yet to experience a passionate beauty professional, and I've found that once they do encounter that sort of passion, they're happy to pay for it.

I referred a woman I met at a networking event to a client's salon because she was telling me that she couldn't find a decent one. She was sick of the very ordinary service she was getting. Months later I bumped into her again, and she was busting to tell me that although she now pays double, she loves her visits to see the guys I recommended.

She said "It's a pleasure to watch people who genuinely love what they do." I have to say, she looked great!

I never said "I am going to work" – EVER! I always said I was going to the salon. Love what you do and you will never work a day in your life.

You need to understand that this is not a desk job. It's a job in which you have to be on top of your game every single day. Your clients react to how you are emotionally. Yes, it's a big ask, but I think it's the most rewarding thing that you could be doing. Making people not only look beautiful – but also feel beautiful. They love you for it!

> *Love what you do and you will never work a day in your life*

Is that why you bought the salon in the first place? Because you love making people look beautiful? Is it still true today? If it is true and you're still fed up, then maybe it's because your salon isn't as profitable as it needs to be.

If that's the case, then turn back to the money chapters in this book, and see what you can do to get bigger margins, get paid what you are worth, and take the financial stress out of your life.

If you really are sick of it all, then look at what you need to do to make your salon an appealing purchase and work towards that.

Sometimes I think that we lose our passion because we don't have a goal in mind – and working at getting your salon ready to sell might be the impetus you need to reignite your passion for the industry.

For more information and resources head to salonsmarts.work

This is one of many messages that come across Lisa's desk. She loves hearing from you, so drop her a line!

Hi Lisa!

Geez I start like we've met and known each other for ages, when the fact is we have never met.

My name is ▇▇▇ I own a salon based in ▇▇▇ Victoria called ▇▇▇ ▇▇▇ and I wanted to say 'thank you' to you for your amazing book The Naked Salon.

I purchased this book about two weeks ago and have just completed it - yep slow reader - and you have successfully helped me re-ignite the fire in my belly for my salon.

I had recognised I had become complacent with my business (even after spending an insane amount on coaching, implementing some systems and still chasing my friggin' tail), and I was putting my "I need help shoes" on when I stumbled across something on Facebook regarding your book and that was it -my sign- that's what I needed. Best $$ spent so far!

So thank you!

Now, recognising that I need assistance, I would love it if I could arrange a meeting with you or one of your team to help me with my business.

I am scared to say it and face it (though I have to if I am to move forward): I feel I am failing and for me failure is not an option - nor is bowing out. I started my business to change something within the industry, to give people something they haven't had before, and to also show the world I can stand on my own two little feet. So, this being said, I'd love to hear from you or the Zing team and see if we can play shop together?

Thank you again for understanding the business owner, the industry, for writing your book and simply understanding just how shit works :)

Regards,

PS: If this is the weirdest email you've received, my apologies - it's my way of saying what I mean and meaning what I say!

Have a great day.

Find out how to take your salon from Good to GREAT!

www.ingramcontent.com/pod-product-compliance
Lightning Source LLC
Chambersburg PA
CBHW050306010526
44107CB00055B/2128